A Buddhist Bible

ISBN: 978 1 8647653 1 1

AXIOM
AUSTRALIA

www.axiompublishing.com.au

Printed in Malaysia

A
Buddhist Bible

Dwight Goddard

Contents

Introduction

As an extended introduction to the study of Lankavatra Sutra has been given by Prof. Suzuki in both his studies and translation, only a very brief statement is necessary here.

Nothing is known as to its author, the time of its composition, or as to its original form. There is a myth that it originally consisted of 100,000 verses, and the second chapter of the present text has a footnote which reads: "Here ends the second chapter of the Collection of all the Dharmas, taken from the Lankavatara of 36,000 verses." Apparently it was originally a collection of verses covering all the main teachings of Mahayana Buddhism. This vast collection of verses became a source from which the Masters selected texts for their discourses. As the verses were very epigrammatic, obscure and disconnected, in the course of time the discourses were remembered and the verses largely forgotten, until in the present text there are remaining only 884 verses. The present text has every appearance of being something in the way of a disciple's notebook in which he had written down extracts or outlines of his master's discourses on some of these verses.

It is generally felt that the present text must have been compiled early in the First Century, probably a little earlier than the AWAKENING OF FAITH by Ashvagosha, which doctrinally it greatly resembles. The earliest date connected with it is the date of the first Chinese translation made by Dharmaraksha about A.D. 420 and which was lost before 700. Three other Chinese translations have been made: one by Gunabhadra in 443; one by Bodhiruci in 513; and one by Shikshananda about 700. There is also one Tibetan version.

The Sutra has always been a favorite with the Ch'an Sect (Zen, in Japan) and has had a great deal to do with that sect's origin and development. There is a tradition that when Bodhidharma handed over his begging-bowl and robe to his successor that he also gave him his copy of the Lankavatara, saying, that he needed no other sutra. In the early days of the Ch'an Sect the Sutra was very much studied, but because of its difficulties and obscurities it gradually dropped out of common use and has been very much neglected for the past thousand years. But during that time many of the great Masters have made it a subject of study and many commentaries have been written upon it. Although other sutras have been more commonly read none have been more influential in fixing the general doctrines of Mahayana Buddhism, and in bringing about the general adoption of Buddhism in China, Korea and Japan.

In closing just a paragraph must be given about the characteristic teachings of the LANKAVATARA. It is not written as a philosophical treatise is written, to establish a certain system of thought, but was written to elucidate the profoundest experience that comes to the human spirit. It everywhere deprecates dependence upon words and doctrines and urges upon all the wisdom of making a determined effort to attain this highest experience. Again and again it repeats with variations the refrain: "Mahamati, you and all the Bodhisattva-Mahasattvas should avoid the erroneous reasonings of the philosophers and seek this self-realisation of Noble Wisdom." For this reason the LANKAVATARA is to be classed with the intuitional scriptures of the Orient, rather than with the philosophical literature of the Occident. In China it combined easily with the accepted belief of the Chinese in Laotsu's conception of the Tao and its ethical idealism to make the Buddhism of China and Japan eminently austere and practical, rather than philosophical and emotional.

Chapter I

Discrimination

THUS HAVE I HEARD. The Blessed One once appeared in the Castle of Lanka which is on the summit of Mt. Malaya in the midst of the great Ocean. A great many Bodhisattva-Mahasattvas had miraculously assembled from all the Buddha-lands, and a large number of bhikshus were gathered there. The Bodhisattva-Mahasattvas with Mahamati at their head were all perfect masters of the various Samadhis, the tenfold Self-mastery, the ten Powers, and the six Psychic Faculties. Having been anointed by the Buddha's own hands, they all well understood the significance of the objective world; they all knew how to apply the various means, teachings and disciplinary measures according to the various mentalities and behaviors of beings; they were all thoroughly versed in the five Dharmas, the three Svabhavas, the eight Vijnanas, and the twofold Egolessness.

The Blessed One, knowing of the mental agitations going on in the minds of those assembled (like the surface of the ocean stirred into waves by the passing winds), and his great heart moved by compassion, smiled and said: In the days of old the Tathagatas of the past who were Arhats and fully-enlightened Ones came to the Castle of Lanka on Mount Malaya and discoursed on the Truth of Noble Wisdom that is beyond the reasoning knowledge of the philosophers as well as being beyond the understanding of ordinary disciples and masters; and which is realisable only within the inmost consciousness; for your sakes, I too, would discourse on the same Truth. All that is seen in the world is devoid of effort and action because all things in the world are like a dream, or like an image miraculously projected. This is not comprehended by the philosophers and the ignorant, but those who thus see things see them truthfully. Those who see things otherwise walk in discrimination and, as they depend upon discrimination, they cling to dualism. The world as seen by discrimination is like seeing one's own image reflected in a mirror, or one's shadow, or the moon reflected in water, or an echo heard in the valley. People grasping their own shadows of discrimination become attached to this thing and that thing and failing to abandon dualism they go on forever discriminating and thus never attain tranquillity. By tranquillity is meant Oneness, and Oneness gives birth to the highest Samadhi which is gained by entering into the realm of Noble Wisdom that is realisable only within one's inmost consciousness.

Then all the Bodhisattva-Mahasattvas rose from their seats and respectfully paid him homage and Mahamati the Bodhisattva-Mahasattva sustained by the power of the Buddhas drew his upper garment over one shoulder, knelt and pressing his hands together, praised him in the following verses:

As thou reviewest the world with thy perfect intelligence and compassion, it must seem to thee like an ethereal flower of which one cannot say: it is born, it is destroyed, for the terms being and non-being do not apply to it.

As thou reviewest the world with thy perfect intelligence and compassion, it must seem to thee like a dream of which it cannot be said: it is permanent or it is destructible, for being and non-being do not apply to it.

As thou reviewest all things by thy perfect intelligence and compassion, they must seem to thee like visions beyond the reach of the human mind, as being and non-being do not apply to them.

With thy perfect intelligence and compassion which are beyond all limit, thou comprehendest the egolessness of things and persons, and art free and clear from the hindrances of passion and learning and egotism.

Thou dost not vanish into Nirvana. nor does Nirvana abide in thee, for Nirvana transcends all duality of knowing and known, of being and non-being.

Those who see thee thus, serene and beyond conception, will be emancipated from attachment, will be cleansed of all defilement, both in this world and in the spiritual world beyond.

In this world whose nature is like a dream, there is place for praise and blame, but in the ultimate Reality of Dharmakaya which is far beyond the senses and the discriminating mind, what is there to praise? O thou most Wise!

THEN SAID MAHAMATI the Bodhisattva-Mahasattva: O blessed One, Sugata, Arhat and Fully-enlightened One, pray tell us about the realisation of Noble Wisdom which is beyond the path and usage of the philosophers; which is devoid of all predicates such as being and non-being, oneness and otherness, bothness and not-bothness, existence and non-existence, eternity and non-eternity; which has nothing to do with individuality and generality, nor false-imagination, nor any illusions arising from the mind itself; but which manifests itself as the Truth of Highest Reality. By which, going up continuously by the stages of purification, one enters at last upon the stage of Tathagatahood, whereby, by the power of his original vows unattended by any striving, one will radiate its influence to infinite worlds, like a gem reflecting its variegated colors, whereby I and other Bodhisattva-Mahasattvas, will be enabled to bring all beings to the same perfection of virtue.

Said the Blessed One: Well done, well done, Mahamati! And again, well done, indeed! It is because of your compassion for the world, because of the benefit it will bring to many people both human kind and celestial, that you have presented yourself before us to make this request. Therefore, Mahamati, listen well and truly reflect upon what I shall say, for I will instruct you.

Then Mahamati and the other Bodhisattva-Mahasattvas gave devout attention to the teaching of the Blessed One.

Mahamati, since the ignorant and simple-minded, not knowing that the world is only something seen of the mind itself, cling to the multitudinousness of external objects, cling to the notions of being and nonbeing, oneness and otherness, bothness and not-bothness, existence and non-existence, eternity and non-eternity, and think that they have a self-nature of their own, all of which rises from the discriminations of the mind and is perpetuated by habit-energy, and from which they are given over to false imagination. It is all like a mirage in which springs of water are seen as if they were real. They are thus imagined by animals who, made thirsty by the heat of the season, run after them. Animals, not knowing that the springs are an hallucination of their own minds, do not realise that there are no such springs. In the same way, Mahamati, the ignorant and simple-minded, their minds burning with the fires of greed, anger and folly, finding delight in a world of multitudinous forms, their thoughts obsessed with ideas of birth, growth and destruction, not well understanding what is meant by existent and non-existent, and being impressed by the erroneous discriminations and speculations since beginningless time, fall into the habit of grasping this and that and thereby becoming attached to them.

It is like the city of the Gandharvas which the unwitting take to be a real city though it is not so in fact. The city appears as in a vision owing to their attachment to the memory of a city preserved in the mind as a seed; the city can thus be said to be both existent and non-existent. In the same way, clinging to the memory of erroneous speculations and doctrines accumulated since beginningless time, they hold fast to such ideas as oneness and otherness, being and nonbeing, and their thoughts are not at all clear as to what after all is only seen of the mind. It is like a man dreaming in his sleep of a country that seems to be filled with various men, women, elephants, horses, cars, pedestrians, villages, towns, hamlets, cows, buffalos, mansions, woods, mountains, rivers and lakes, and who moves about in that city until he is awakened. As he lies half awake, he recalls the city of his dreams and reviews his experiences there; what do you think, Mahamati, is this dreamer who is letting his mind dwell upon the various unrealities he has seen in his dream,—is he to be considered wise or foolish? In the same way, the ignorant and simple-minded who are favorably influenced by the erroneous views of the philosophers do not recognise that the views that are influencing them are only dream-like ideas originating in the mind itself, and consequently they are held fast by their notions of oneness and otherness, of being and non-being. It is like a painter's canvas on which the ignorant imagine they see the elevations and depressions of mountains and valleys.

In the same way there are people today being brought up under the influence of similar erroneous views of oneness and otherness, of bothness and not-bothness, whose mentality is being conditioned by the habit-energy of these false-imaginings and who later on will declare those who hold the true doctrine of no-birth which is free from the alternatives of being and non-being, to be nihilists and by so doing will bring themselves and others to ruin. By the natural law of cause and effect these followers of pernicious views uproot meritorious causes that otherwise would lead to unstained purity. They are to be shunned by those whose desires are for more excellent things.

It is like the dim-eyed ones who seeing a hairnet exclaim to one another: "It is wonderful! Look, Honorable Sirs, it is wonderful!" But the hairnet has never existed; in fact, it is neither an entity, nor a nonentity, for it has both been seen and has not been seen. in the same manner those whose minds have been addicted to the discriminations of the erroneous views cherished by the philosophers which are given over to the realistic views of being and non-being, will contradict the good Dharma and will end in the destruction of themselves and others.

It is like a wheel of fire made by a revolving firebrand which is no wheel but which is imagined to be one by the ignorant. Nor is it not-a-wheel because it has not been seen by some. By the same reasoning, those who are in the habit of listening to the discriminations and views of the philosophers will regard things born as non-existent and those destroyed by causation as existent. It is like a mirror reflecting colors and images as determined by conditions but without any partiality. It is like the echo of the wind that gives the sound of a human voice. It is like a mirage of moving water seen in a desert. In the same way the discriminating mind of the ignorant which has been heated by false-imaginations and speculations is stirred into mirage-like waves by the winds of birth, growth and destruction. It is like the magician Pisaca, who by means of his spells makes a wooden image or a dead body to throb with life, though it has no power of its own. In the same way the ignorant and the simpleminded, committing themselves to erroneous philosophical views become thoroughly devoted to the ideas of oneness and otherness, but their confidence is not well-grounded. For this reason, Mahamati, you and other Bodhisattva-Mahasattvas should cast off all discriminations leading to the notions of birth, abiding and destructions, of oneness and otherness, of bothness and not-bothness, of being and non-being and thus getting free of the bondage of habit-energy become able to attain the reality realisable within yourselves of Noble Wisdom.

THEN SAID MAHAMATI to the Blessed One: Why is it that the ignorant are given up to discrimination and the wise are not?

The Blessed One replied: It is because the ignorant cling to names, signs and ideas; as their minds move along these channels they feed on multiplicities of objects and fall into the notion of an ego-soul and what belongs to it; they make discriminations of good and bad among appearances and cling to the agreeable. As they thus cling there is a reversion to ignorance, and karma born of greed, anger and folly, is accumulated. As the accumulation of karma goes on they become imprisoned in a cocoon of discrimination and are thenceforth unable to free themselves from the round of birth and death.

Because of folly they do not understand that all things are like maya, like the reflection of the moon in water, that there is no self-substance to be imagined as an ego-soul and its belongings, and that all their definitive ideas rise from their false discriminations of what exists only as it is seen of the mind itself. They do not realise that things have nothing to do with qualified and qualifying, nor with the course of birth, abiding and destruction, and instead they assert that they are born of a creator, of time, of atoms, of some celestial spirit. It is because the ignorant are given up to discrimination that they move along with the stream of appearances, but it is not so with the wise.

Chapter II

False-Imagination and Knowledge of Appearances

THEN MAHAMATI the Bodhisattva-Mahasattva spoke to the Blessed One, saying: You speak of the erroneous views of the philosophers, will you please tell us of them, that we may be on our guard against them?

The Blessed One replied, saying: Mahamati, the error in these erroneous teachings that are generally held by the philosophers lies in this: they do not recognise that the objective world rises from the mind itself; they do not understand that the whole mind-system also rises from the mind itself; but depending upon these manifestations of the mind as being real they go on discriminating them, like the simple-minded ones that they are, cherishing the dualism of this and that, of being and non-being, ignorant of the fact that there is but one common Essence.

On the contrary my teaching is based upon the recognition that the objective world, like a vision, is a manifestation of the mind itself; it teaches the cessation of ignorance, desire, deed and causality; it teaches the cessation of suffering that arises from the discriminations of the triple world.

There are some Brahman scholars who, assuming something out of nothing, assert that there is a substance bound up with causation which abides in time, and that the elements that make up personality and its environment have their genesis and continuation in causation and after thus existing, pass away. Then there are other scholars who hold a destructive and nihilistic view concerning such subjects as continuation, activity, breaking-up, existence, Nirvana, the Path, karma, fruition and Truth. Why? Because they have not attained an intuitive understanding of Truth itself and therefore they have no clear insight into the fundamentals of things. They are like a jar broken into pieces which is no longer able to function as a jar; they are like a burnt seed which is no longer capable of sprouting. But the elements that make up personality and its environment which they regard as subject to change are really incapable of uninterrupted transformations. Their views are based upon erroneous discriminations of the objective world; they are not based upon the true conception.

Again, if it is true that something comes out of nothing and there is the rise of the mind-system by reason of the combination of the three effect-producing causes, we could say the same of any non-existing thing: for instance, that a tortoise could grow hair, or sand produce oil. This proposition is of no avail; it ends in affirming nothing. It follows that the deed, work and cause of which they speak is of no use, and so also is their reference to being and non-being. If they argue that there is a combination of the three effect-producing causes, they must do it on the principle of cause and effect, that is, that something comes out of something and not out of nothing. As long as a world of relativity is asserted, there is an ever recurring chain of causation which cannot be denied under any circumstance, therefore we cannot talk of anything coming to an end or of cessation. As long as these scholars remain on their philosophical ground their demonstration must conform to logic and their textbooks, and the memory-habit of erroneous intellection will ever cling to them. To make the matter worse, the simple-minded ones, poisoned by this erroneous view, will declare this incorrect way of thinking taught by the ignorant, to be the same as that presented by the All-knowing One.

But the way of instruction presented by the Tathagatas is not based on assertions and refutations by means of words and logic. There are four forms of assertion that can be made concerning things not in existence, namely, assertions made about individual marks that are not in existence; about objects that are not in existence; about a cause that is non-existent; and about philosophical views that are erroneous. By refutation is meant that one, because of ignorance, has not examined properly the error that lies at the base of these assertions.

The assertion about individual marks that really have no existence, concerns the distinctive marks as perceived by the eye, ear, nose, etc., as indicating individuality and generality in the elements that make up personality and its external world; and then, taking these marks for reality and getting attached to them, to get into the habit of affirming that things are just so and not otherwise.

The assertion about objects that are non-existent is an assertion that rises from attachment to these associated marks of individuality and generality. Objects in themselves are neither in existence nor in non-existence and are quite devoid of the alternative of being and non-being, and should only be thought of as one thinks of the horns of a hare, a horse, or a camel, which never existed. Objects are discriminated by the ignorant who are addicted to assertion and negation, because their intelligence has not been acute enough to penetrate into the truth that there is nothing but what is seen of the mind itself.

The assertion of a cause that is non-existent assumes the causeless birth of the first element of the mind-system which later on comes to have only a maya-like non-existence. That is to say, there are philosophers who assert that an originally un-born mind-system begins to function under the conditions of eye, form, light and memory, which functioning goes on for a time and then ceases. This is an example of a cause that is non-existent.

The assertion of philosophical views concerning the elements that make up personality and its environing world that are non-existent, assume the existence of an ego, a being, a soul, a living being, a "nourisher," or a spirit. This is an example of philosophical views that are not true. It is this combination of discrimination of imaginary marks of individuality, grouping them and giving them a name and becoming attached to them as objects, by reason of habit-energy that has been accumulating since beginningless time, that one builds up erroneous views whose only basis is false-imagination. For this reason Bodhisattvas should avoid all discussions relating to assertions and negations whose only basis is words and logic.

Word-discrimination goes on by the coordination of brain, chest, nose, throat, palate, lips, tongue, teeth and lips. Words are neither different nor not-different from discrimination. Words rise from discrimination as their cause; if words were different from discrimination they could not have discrimination for their cause; then again, if words are not different, they could not carry and express meaning. Words, therefore, are produced by causation and are mutually conditioning and shifting and, just like things, are subject to birth and destruction.

There are four kinds of word discrimination, all of which are to be avoided because they are alike unreal. First there are the words indicating individual marks which rise from discriminating forms and signs as being real in themselves and, then, becoming attached to them. There are memory-words which rise from the unreal surroundings which come before the mind when it recalls some previous experience. Then there are words growing out of attachment to the erroneous distinctions and speculations of the mental processes. And finally, there are words growing out of inherited prejudices as seeds of habit-energy have accumulated since beginningless time, or which had their origin in some long forgotten clinging to false-imagination and erroneous speculations.

Then there are words where there are no corresponding objects, as for instance, the hare's horns, a barren woman's child, etc.—there are no such things but we have the words, just the same. Words are an artificial creation; there are Buddha-lands where there are no words. In some Buddha-lands ideas are indicated by looking steadily, in others by gestures, in still others by a frown, by a movement of the eyes, by laughing, by yawning, by the clearing of the throat, or by trembling. For instance, in the Buddha-land of the Tathagata Samantabhadra, Bodhisattvas, by a dhyana transcending words and ideas, attain the recognition of all things as un-born and they, also, experience various most excellent Samadhis that transcend words. Even in this world such specialised beings as ants and bees carry on their activities very well without recourse to words. No, Mahamati, the validity of things is independent of the validity of words.

Moreover, there are other things that belong to words, namely, the syllable-body of words, the name-body of words, and the sentence-body of words. By. syllable-body is meant that by which words and sentences are set up or indicated: there is a reason for some syllables, some are mnemonic, and some are chosen arbitrarily. By name-body is meant the object depending upon which a name-word obtains its significance, or in other words, name-body is the "substance" of a name-word. By sentence-body is meant the completion of the meaning by expressing the word more fully in a sentence. The name for this sentence-body is suggested by the footprints left in the road by elephants, horses, people, deer, cattle, goats, etc. But neither words nor sentences can exactly express meanings, for words are only sweet sounds that are arbitrarily chosen to represent things, they are not the things themselves, which in turn are only manifestations of mind. Discrimination of meaning is based upon the false-imagination that these sweet sounds which we call words and which are dependent upon whatever subjects they are supposed to stand for, and which subjects are supposed to be self-existent, all of which is based on error. Disciples should be on their guard against the seductions of words and sentences and their illusive meanings, for by them the ignorant and the dull-witted become entangled and helpless as an elephant floundering about in the deep mud.

Words and sentences are produced by the law of causation and are mutually conditioning—they cannot express highest Reality. Moreover, in highest Reality there are no differentiations to be discriminated and there is nothing to be predicated in regard to it. Highest Reality is an exalted state of bliss, it is not a state of word-discrimination and it cannot be entered into by mere statements concerning it. The Tathagatas have a better way of teaching, namely, through self-realisation of Noble Wisdom.

MAHAMATI ASKED the Blessed One: Pray tell us about the causation of all things whereby I and other Bodhisattvas may see into the nature of causation and may no more discriminate it as to the gradual or simultaneous rising of all things?

The Blessed One replied: There are two factors of causation by reason of which all things come into seeming existence:—external and internal factors. The external factors are a lump of clay, a stick, a wheel, a thread, water, a worker, and his labor, the combination of all of which produces a jar. As with a jar which is made from a lump of clay, or a piece of cloth made from thread, or matting made from fragrant grass, or a sprout growing out of a seed, or fresh butter made from sour milk by a man churning it; so it is with all things which appear one after another in continuous succession. As regards the inner factors of causation, they are of such kinds as ignorance, desire, purpose, all of which enter into the idea of causation. Born of these two factors there is the manifestation of personality and the individual things that make up its environment, but they are not individual and distinctive things: they are only so discriminated by the ignorant.

Causation may be divided into six elements: indifference-cause, dependence-cause, possibility-cause, agency-cause, objectivity-cause, manifesting-cause. Indifference-cause means that if there is no discrimination present, there is no power of combination present and so no combination takes place, or if present there is dissolution. Dependence-cause means that the elements must be present. Possibility-cause means that when a cause is to become effective there must be a suitable meeting of conditions both internal and external. Agency-cause means that there must be a principle vested with supreme authority like a sovereign king present and asserting itself. Objectivity-cause means that to be a part of the objective world the mind-system must be in existence and must be keeping up its continuous activity. Manifesting-cause means that as the discriminating faculty of the mind-system becomes busy individual marks will be revealed as forms are revealed by the light of a lamp.

All causes are thus seen to be the outcome of discrimination carried on by the ignorant and simple-minded, and there is, therefore, no such thing as gradual or simultaneous rising of existence. If such a thing as the gradual rising of existence is asserted, it can be disproved by showing that there is no basic substance to hold the individual signs together which makes a gradual rising impossible. If simultaneous rising of existence is asserted, there would be no distinction between cause and effect and there will be nothing to characterise a cause as such. While a child is not yet born, the term father has no significance. Logicians argue that there is that which is born and that which gives birth by the mutual functioning of such causal factors as cause, substance, continuity, acceleration, etc., and so they conclude that there is a gradual rising of existence; but this gradual rising does not obtain except by reason of attachment to the notion of self-nature.

When ideas of body, property and abode are seen, discriminated and cherished in what after all is nothing but what is conceived by the mind itself, an external world is perceived under the aspects of individuality and generality which, however, are not realities, and, therefore, neither a gradual nor a simultaneous rising of things is possible. It is only when the mind-system comes into activity and discriminates the manifestations of mind that existence can be said to come into view. For these reasons, Mahamati, you must get rid of notions of gradation and simultaneity in the combination of causal activities.

MAHAMATI SAID: Blessed One, To what kind of discrimination and to what kind of thoughts should the term, false-imagination, be applied?

The Blessed One replied: So long as people do not understand the true nature of the objective world, they fall into the dualistic view of things. They imagine the multiplicity of external objects to be real and become attached to them and are nourished by their habit-energy. Because of this a system of mentation—mind and what belongs to it—is discriminated and is thought of as real; this leads to the assertion of an ego-soul and its belongings, and thus the mind-system goes on functioning. Depending upon and attaching itself to the dualistic habit of mind, they accept the views of the philosophers founded upon these erroneous distinctions, of being and non-being, existence and non-existence, and there evolves what we call, false-imaginations.

But, Mahamati, discrimination does not evolve nor is it put away because, when all that is seen is truly recognised to be nothing but the manifestation of mind, how can discrimination as regards being and non-being evolve? It is for the sake of the ignorant who are addicted to the discrimination of the multiplicity of things which are of their own mind, that it is said by me that discrimination takes its rise owing to attachment to the aspect of multiplicity which is characteristic of objects. How otherwise can the ignorant and simple-minded recognize that there is nothing but what is seen of the mind itself, and how otherwise can they gain an insight into the true nature of mind and be able to free themselves from wrong conceptions of cause and effect? How otherwise can they gain a clear conception of the Bodhisattva stages, and attain a "turning-about" in the deepest seat of their consciousness, and finally attain an inner self-realisation of Noble Wisdom which transcends the five Dharmas, the three Self-natures, and the whole idea of a discriminated Reality? For this reason is it said by me that discrimination takes its rise from the mind becoming attached to the multiplicities of things which in themselves are not real, and that emancipation comes from thoroughly understanding the meaning of Reality as it truly is.

False-imaginations rise from the consideration of appearances: things are discriminated as to form, signs and shape; as to having color, warmth, humidity, motility or rigidity. False-imagination consists in becoming attached to these appearances and their names. By attachment to objects is meant, the getting attached to inner and outer things as if they were real. By attachment to names is meant, the recognition in these inner and outer things of the characteristic marks of individuation and generality, and to regard them as definitely belonging to the names of the objects.

False-imagination teaches that because all things are bound up with causes and conditions of habit-energy that has been accumulating since beginningless time by not recognising that the external world is of mind itself, all things are comprehensible under the aspects of individuality and generality. By reason of clinging to these false-imaginations there is multitudinousness of appearances which are imagined to be real but which are only imaginary. To illustrate: when a magician depending on grass, wood, shrubs and creepers, exercises his art, many shapes and beings take form that are only magically created; sometimes they even make figures that have bodies and that move and act like human beings; they are variously and fancifully discriminated but there is no reality in them; everyone but children and the simple-minded know that they are not real. Likewise based upon the notion of relativity false-imagination perceives a variety of appearances which the discriminating mind proceeds to objectify and name and become attached to, and memory and habit-energy perpetuate. Here is all that is necessary to constitute the self-nature of false-imagination.

The various features of false-imagination can be distinguished as follows: as regards words, meaning, individual marks, property, self-nature, cause, philosophical views, reasoning, birth, no-birth, dependence, bondage and emancipation. Discrimination of words is the becoming attached to various sounds carrying familiar meanings. Discrimination of meaning comes when one imagines that words rise depending upon whatever subjects they express, and which subjects are regarded as self-existent. Discrimination of individual marks is to imagine that whatever is denoted in words concerning the multiplicities of individual marks (which in themselves are like a mirage) is true, and clinging tenaciously to them, to discriminate all things according to such categories as, warmth, fluidity, motility, and solidity. Discrimination of property is to desire a state of wealth, such as gold, silver, and various precious stories.

Discrimination of self-nature is to make discriminations according to the views of the philosophers in reference to the self-nature of all things which they imagine and stoutly maintain to be true, saying: "This is just what it is and it cannot be otherwise." Discrimination of cause is to distinguish the notion of causation in reference to being and non-being and to imagine that there are such things as "cause-signs." Discrimination of philosophical views means considering different views relating to the notions of being and nonbeing, oneness and otherness, bothness and not-bothness, existence and non-existence, all of which are erroneous, and becoming attached to particular views. Discrimination of reasoning means the teaching whose reasoning is based on the grasping of the notion of an ego-substance and what belongs to it. Discrimination of birth means getting attached to the notion that things come into existence and pass out of existence according to causation. Discrimination of no-birth is to see that causeless substances which were not, come into existence by reason of causation. Discrimination of dependence means the mutual dependence of gold and the filament made of it. Discrimination of bondage and imagination is like imagining that there is something bound because of something binding, as in the case of a man who ties a knot and loosens one.

These are the various features of false-imagination to which all the ignorant and simple-minded cling. Those attached to the notion of relativity are attached to the notion of the multitudinousness of things which arises from false-imagination. It is like seeing varieties of objects depending upon maya, but these varieties thus revealing themselves are discriminated by the ignorant as something other than maya itself, according to their way of thinking. Now the truth is, maya and varieties of objects are neither different nor not different; if they were different, varieties of objects would not have maya for their characteristic; if they are not different there would be no distinction between them. But as there is a distinction these two—maya and varieties of objects-are neither different nor not-different, for the very good reason: they are one thing.

MAHAMATI SAID to the Blessed One: Is error an entity or not? The Blessed One replied: Error has no character in it making for attachment; if error had such a character no liberation would be possible from its attachment to existence, and the chain of origination would only be understood in the sense of creation as upheld by the philosophers. Error is like maya, also, and as maya is incapable from producing other maya, so error in itself cannot produce error; it is discrimination and attachment that produce evil thoughts and faults. Moreover, maya has no power of discrimination in itself; it only rises when invoked by the charm of the magician. Error has in itself no habit-energy; habit-energy only rises from discrimination and attachment. Error in itself has no faults; faults are due to the confused discriminations fondly cherished by the ignorant concerning the ego-soul and its mind. The wise have nothing to do either with maya or error.

Maya, however, is not an unreality because it only has the appearance of reality; all things have the nature of maya. It is not because all things are imagined and clung to because of the multitudinous of individual signs, that they are like maya; it is because they are alike unreal and as quickly appearing and disappearing. Being attached to erroneous thoughts they confuse and contradict themselves and others. As they do not clearly grasp the fact that the world is no more than mind itself, they imagine and cling to causation, work, birth and individual signs, and their thoughts are characterised by error and false-imaginations. The teaching that all things are characterised by the self-nature of maya and a dream is meant to make the ignorant and simple-minded cast aside the idea of self-nature in anything.

False-imagination teaches that such things as light and shade, long and short, black and white are different and are to be discriminated; but they are not independent of each other; they are only different aspects of the same thing, they are terms of relation not of reality. Conditions of existence are not of a mutually exclusive character; in essence things are not two but one. Even Nirvana and Samsara's world of life and death are aspects of the same thing, for there is no Nirvana except where is Samasara, and no Samsara except where is Nirvana. All duality is falsely imagined.

Mahamati, you and all the Bodhisattvas should discipline yourselves in the realisation and patient acceptance of the truths of the emptiness, un-bornness, no self-natureness, and the non-duality of all things. This teaching is found in all the sutras of all the Buddhas and is presented to meet the varied dispositions of all beings, but it is not the Truth itself. These teachings are only a finger pointing toward Noble Wisdom. They are like a mirage with its springs of water which the deer take to be real and chase after. So with the teachings in all the sutras: They are intended for the consideration and guidance of the discriminating minds of all people, but they are not the Truth itself, which can only be self-realised within one's deepest consciousness.

Mahamati, you and all the Bodhisattvas must seek for this inner self-realisation of Noble Wisdom, and be not captivated by word-teaching.

Chapter III

Right Knowledge or Knowledge of Relations

THEN MAHAMATI SAID: Pray tell us, Blessed One, about the being and the non-being of all things?

The Blessed One replied: People of this world are dependent in their thinking on one of two things: on the notion of being whereby they take pleasure in realism, or in the notion of non-being whereby they take pleasure in nihilism; in either case they imagine emancipation where there is no emancipation. Those who are dependent upon the notion of being, regard the world as rising from a causation that is really existent, and that this actually existing and becoming world does not take its rise from a causation that is non-existent. This is the realistic view as held by some people. Then there are other people who are dependent on the notion of the non-being of all things. These people admit the existence of greed, anger and folly, and at the same time they deny the existence of the things that produce greed, anger and folly. This is not rational, for greed, anger and folly are no more to be taken hold of as real than are things; they neither have substance nor individual marks. Where there is a state of bondage, there is binding and means for binding; but where there is emancipation, as in the case of Buddhas, Bodhisattvas, masters and disciples, who have ceased to believe in both being and non-being, there is neither bondage, binding nor means for binding.

It is better to cherish the notion of an ego-substance than to entertain the notion of emptiness derived from the view of being and non-being, for those who so believe fail to understand the, fundamental fact that the external world is nothing but a manifestation of mind. Because they see things as, transient, as rising from cause and passing away from cause, now dividing, now combining into the elements which make up the aggregates of personality and its external world and now passing away, they are doomed to suffer every moment from the changes that follow one after another, and finally are doomed to ruin.

THEN MAHAMATI ASKED the Blessed One, saying: Tell us, Blessed One, how all things can be empty, un-born, and have no self-nature, so that we may be awakened and quickly realise highest enlightenment?

The Blessed One replied: What is emptiness, indeed! It is a term whose very self-nature is false-imagination, but because of one's attachment to false-imagination we are obliged to talk of emptiness, no-birth, and no-self-nature. There are seven kinds of emptiness: emptiness of mutuality which is non-existence; emptiness of individual marks; emptiness of self-nature; emptiness of no-work; emptiness of work; emptiness of all things in the sense that they are unpredicable; and emptiness in its highest sense of Ultimate Reality.

By the emptiness of mutuality which is non-existence is meant that when a thing is missing here, one speaks of its being empty here. For instance: in the lecture hall of Mrigarama there are no elephants present, nor bulls, nor sheep; but as to monks there are many present. We can rightly speak of the hall as being empty as far as animals are concerned. It is not asserted that the lecture hall is empty of its own characteristics, or that the monks are empty of that which makes up their monkhood, nor that in some other place there are no elephants, bulls, nor sheep to be found. In this case we are speaking of things in their aspect of individuality and generality, but from the point of view of mutuality some things do not exist somewhere. This is the lowest form of emptiness and is to be sedulously put away.

By emptiness of individual marks is meant that all things have no distinguishing marks of individuality and generality. Because of mutual relations and interactions things are superficially discriminated but when they are further and more carefully investigated and analysed they are seen to be non-existent and nothing as to individuality and generality can be predicated of them. Thus when individual marks can no longer be seen, ideas of self, otherness and bothness, no longer hold good. So it must be said that all things are empty of self-marks.

By emptiness of self-nature is meant that all things in their self-nature are un-born; therefore, is it said that things are empty as to self-nature. By emptiness of no-work is meant that the aggregate of elements that makes up personality and its external world is Nirvana itself and from the beginning there is no activity in them; therefore, one speaks of the emptiness of no-work. By emptiness of work is meant that the aggregates being devoid of an ego and its belongings, go on functioning automatically as there is mutual conjunction of. causes and conditions; thus one speaks of the emptiness of work. By emptiness of all things in the sense that they are unpredicable is meant that, as the very nature of false-imagination is inexpressible, so all things are unpredicable, and, therefore, are empty in that sense. By emptiness in its highest sense of the emptiness of Ultimate Reality is meant that in the attainment of inner self-realisation of Noble Wisdom there is no trace of habit-energy generated by erroneous conceptions; thus one speaks of the highest emptiness of Ultimate Reality.

When things are examined by right knowledge there are no signs obtainable which would characterise them with marks of individuality and generality, therefore, they are said to have no self-nature. Because these signs of individuality and generality are seen both as existing and yet are known to be non-existent, are seen as going out and yet are known not to be going out, they are never annihilated. Why is this true? For this reason; because the individual signs that should make up the self-nature of all things are non-existent. Again in their self-nature things are both eternal and non-eternal. Things are not eternal because the marks of individuality appear and disappear, that is, the marks of self-nature are characterised by non-eternality. On the other hand, because things are un-born and are only mind-made, they are in a deep sense eternal. That is, things are eternal because of their very non-eternality.

Further, besides understanding the emptiness of all things both in regard to substance and self-nature, it is necessary for Bodhisattvas to clearly understand that all things are un-born. It is not asserted that things are not born in a superficial sense, but that in a deep sense they are not born of themselves. All that can be said, is this, that relatively speaking, there is a constant stream of becoming, a momentary and uninterrupted change from one state of appearance to another. When it is recognised that the world as it presents itself is no more than a manifestation of mind, then birth is seen as no-birth and all existing objects, concerning which discrimination asserts that they are and are not, are non-existent and, therefore, un-born; being devoid of agent and action things are un-born.

If things are not born of being and non-being, but are simply manifestations of mind itself, they have no reality, no self-nature:—they are like the horns of a hare, a horse, a donkey, a camel. But the ignorant and the simple-minded, who are given over to their false and erroneous imaginings, discriminate things where they are not. To the ignorant the characteristic marks of the self-nature of body-property-and-abode seem to be fundamental and rooted in the very nature of the mind itself, so they discriminate their multitudinousness and become attached to them.

There are two kinds of attachment: attachment to objects as having self-nature, and attachment to words as having self-nature. The first takes place by not knowing that the external world is only a manifestation of the mind itself; and the second arises from one's clinging to words and names by reason of habit-energy. in the teaching of no-birth, causation is out of place because, seeing that all things are like maya and a dream, one does not discriminate individual signs. That all things are un-born and have no self-nature be-cause they are like maya is asserted to meet the thesis of the philosophers that birth is by causation. They foster the notion that the birth of all things is derived from the concept of being and non-being, and fail to regard it as it truly is,—as caused by attachment to the multitudinousness which arises from discriminations of the mind itself.

Those who believe in the birth of something that has never been in existence and, coming into existence, vanishes away, are obliged to assert that things come to exist and vanish away by causation—such people find no foothold in my teachings. When it is realised that there is nothing born, and nothing passes away, then there is no way to admit being and non-being, and the mind becomes quiescent.

THEN MAHAMATI SAID to the Blessed One: The philosophers declare that the world rises from causal agencies according to a law of causation; they state that their cause is unborn and is not to be annihilated. They mention nine primary elements: Ishvara the Creator, the Creation, atoms, etc., which being elementary are unborn and not to be annihilated. The Blessed One, while teaching that all things are un-born and that there is no annihilation, also declares that the world takes its rise from ignorance, discrimination, attachment, deed, etc., working according to a law of causation. Though the two sets of elements may differ in form and name, there does not appear to be any essential difference between the two positions. If there is anything that is distinctive and superior in the Blessed One's teaching, pray tell us, Blessed One, what it is?

The Blessed One replied: My teaching of no-birth and no-annihilation is not like that of the philosophers, nor is it like their doctrine of birth and impermanency. That to which the philosophers ascribe the characteristic of no-birth and no-annihilation is the self-nature of all things, which causes them to fall into the dualism of being and non-being. My teaching transcends the whole conception of being and non-being; it has nothing to do with birth, abiding and destruction; nor with existence and non-existence. I teach that the multitudinousness of objects have no reality in themselves but are only seen of the mind and, therefore, are of the nature of maya and a dream. I teach the non-existence of things because they carry no signs of any inherent self-nature. It is true that in one sense they are seen and discriminated by the senses as individualised objects; but in another sense, because of the absence of any characteristic marks of self-nature, they are not seen but are only imagined. In one sense they are graspable, but in another sense, they are not graspable. When it is clearly understood that there is nothing in the world but what is seen of the mind itself, discrimination no more rises, and the wise are established in their true abode which is the realm of quietude. The ignorant discriminate and work trying to adjust themselves to external conditions, and are constantly perturbed in mind; unrealities are imagined and discriminated, while realities are unseen and ignored. It is not so with the wise. To illustrate: What the ignorant see is like the magically-created city of the Gandharvas, where children are shown streets and houses, and phantom merchants, and people going in and coming out. This imaginary city with its streets and houses and people going in and coming out, are not thought of as being born or being annihilated, because in their case there is no question as to their existence or non-existence. In like manner, I teach, that there is nothing made nor un-made; that there is nothing that has connection with birth and destruction except as the ignorant cherish falsely imagined notions as to the reality of the external world. When objects are not seen and judged as they truly are in themselves, there is discrimination and clinging to the notions of being and non-being, and individualised self-nature, and. as long as these notions of individuality and self-nature persist, the philosophers are bound to explain the external world by a law of causation. This position raises the question of a first cause which the philosophers meet by asserting that their first cause, Ishvara and the primal elements, are un-born and un-annihilate; which position is without evidence and is irrational.

Ignorant people and worldly philosophers cherish a kind of no-birth, but it is not the no-birth which I teach. I teach the un-bornness of the un-born essence of all things which teaching is established in the minds of the wise by their self-realisation of Noble Wisdom. A ladle, clay, a vessel, a wheel, or seeds, or elements—these are external conditions; ignorance discrimination, attachment, habit, karma,—these are inner conditions. When this entire universe is regarded as concatenation and as nothing else but concatenation, then the mind, by its patient acceptance of the truth that all things are un-born, gains tranquillity.

Chapter IV

Perfect Knowledge,
or Knowledge of Reality

HEN MAHAMATI ASKED the Blessed one: Pray tell us, Blessed One, about the five Dharmas, so that we may fully understand Perfect Knowledge?

The Blessed One replied: The five Dharmas are: appearance, name, discrimination, right-knowledge and Reality. By appearance is meant that which reveals itself to the senses and to the discriminating-mind and is perceived as form, sound, odour, taste, and touch. Out of these appearances ideas are formed, such as clay, water, jar, etc., by which one says: this is such and such a thing and is no other,—this is name. When appearances are contrasted and names compared, as when we say: this is an elephant, this is a horse, a cart, a pedestrian, a man, a woman, or, this is mind and what belongs to it,—the things thus named are said to be discriminated. As these discriminations come to be seen as mutually conditioning, as empty of self-substance, as un-born, and thus come to be seen as they truly are, that is, as manifestations of the mind itself,—this is right-knowledge. By it the wise cease to regard appearances and names as realities.

When appearances and names are put away and all discrimination ceases, that which remains is the true and essential nature of things and, as nothing can be predicated as to the nature of essence, it is called the "Suchness" of Reality. This universal, undifferentiated, inscrutable, "Suchness" is the only Reality but it is variously characterised as Truth, Mind-essence, Transcendental Intelligence, Noble Wisdom, etc. This Dharma of the imagelessness of the Essence-nature of Ultimate Reality is the Dharma which has been proclaimed by all the Buddhas, and when all things are understood in full agreement with it, one is in possession of Perfect Knowledge, and is on his way to the attainment of the Transcendental Intelligence of the Tathagatas.

THEN MAHAMATI SAID to the Blessed One: Are the three self-natures, of things, ideas, and Reality, to be considered as included in the Five Dharmas, or as having their own characteristics complete in themselves.

The Blessed One replied: The three self-natures, the eightfold mind-system, and the twofold egolessness are all included in the Five Dharmas. The self-natures of things, of ideas, and of the sixfold mind-system, correspond with the Dharmas of appearance, name and discrimination; the self-nature of Universal Mind and Reality corresponds to the Dharmas of right-knowledge and "Suchness."

By becoming attached to what is seen of the mind itself, there is an activity awakened which is perpetuated by habit-energy that becomes manifest in the mind-system. From the activities of the mind-system there rises the notion of an ego-soul and its belongings; the discriminations, attachments, and notion of an ego-soul, rising simultaneously like the sun and its rays of light.

By the egolessness of things is meant that the elements that make up the aggregates of personality and its objective world being characterised by the nature of maya and destitute of anything that can be called ego-substance, are therefore un-born and have no self-nature. How can things be said to have an ego-soul? By the egolessness of persons is meant that in the aggregates that make up personality there is no ego-substance, nor anything that is like ego-substance nor that belongs to it. The mind-system, which is the most characteristic mark of personality, originated in ignorance, discrimination, desire and deed; and its activities are perpetuated by perceiving, grasping and becoming attached to objects as if they were real. The memory of these discriminations, desires, attachments and deeds is stored in Universal Mind since beginningless time, and is still being accumulated where it conditions the appearance of personality and its environment and brings about constant change and destruction from moment to moment. The manifestations are like a river, a seed, a lamp, a cloud, the wind; Universal mind in its voraciousness to store up everything, is like a monkey never at rest, like a fly ever in search of food and without partiality, like a fire that is never satisfied, like a water-lifting machine that goes on rolling. Universal mind as defiled by habit-energy is like a magician that causes phantom things and people to appear and move about. A thorough understanding of these things is necessary to an understanding of the egolessness of persons.

There are four kinds of Knowledge: Appearance-knowledge, relative-knowledge, perfect-knowledge, and Transcendental Intelligence. Appearance-knowledge belongs to the ignorant and simple-minded who are addicted to the notion of being and non-being, and who are frightened at the thought of being unborn. It is produced by the concordance of the triple combination and attaches itself to the multiplicities of objects; it is characterised by attainability and accumulation; it is subject to birth and destruction. Appearance-knowledge belongs to word-mongers who revel in discriminations, assertions and negations.

Relative-knowledge belongs to the mind-world of the philosophers. It rises from the mind's ability to consider the relations which appearances bear to each other and to the mind considering them, it rises from the mind's ability to arrange, combine and analyse these relations by its powers of discursive logic and imagination, by reason of which it is able to peer into the meaning and significance of things.

Perfect-knowledge belongs to the world of the Bodhisattvas who recognise that all things are but manifestations of mind; who clearly understand the emptiness, the un-bornness, the egolessness of all things; and who have entered into an understanding of the Five Dharmas, the twofold egolessness, and into the truth of imagelessness. Perfect-knowledge differentiates the

Bodhisattva stages, and is the pathway and the entrance into the exalted state of self-realisation of Noble Wisdom.

Perfect-knowledge (*jnana*) belongs to the Bodhisattvas who are entirely free from the dualisms of being and non-being, no-birth and no-annihilation, all assertions and negations, and who, by reason of self-realisation, have gained an insight into the truths of egolessness and imagelessness. They no longer discriminate the world as subject to causation: they regard the causation that rules the world as something like the fabled city of the Gandharvas. To them the world is like a vision and a dream, it is like the birth and death of a barren-woman's child; to them there is nothing evolving and nothing disappearing.

The wise who cherish Perfect-knowledge, may be divided into three classes: disciples, masters and Arhats. Common disciples are separated from masters as common disciples continue to cherish the notion of individuality and generality; masters rise from common disciples when, forsaking the error of individuality and generality, they still cling to the notion of an ego-soul by reason of which they go off by themselves into retirement and solitude. Arhats rise when the error of all discrimination is realised. Error being discriminated by the wise turns into Truth by virtue of the "turning-about" that takes place within the deepest consciousness. Mind, thus emancipated, enters into perfect self-realisation of Noble Wisdom.

But, Mahamati, if you *assert* that there is such a thing as Noble Wisdom, it no longer holds good, because anything of which something is asserted thereby partakes of the nature of being and is thus characterised with the quality of birth. The very assertion: "All things are un-born" destroys the truthfulness of it. The same is true of the statements: "All things are empty," and "All things have no self-nature,"—both are untenable when put in the form of assertions. But when it is pointed out that all things are like a dream and a vision, it means that in one way things are perceived, and in another way they are not perceived; that is, in ignorance they are perceived but in Perfect-knowledge they are not perceived. All assertions and negations being thought-constructions are un-born. Even the assertion that Universal Mind and Noble Wisdom are Ultimate Reality, is thought construction and, therefore, is un-born. As "things" there is no Universal Mind, there is no Noble Wisdom, there is no Ultimate Reality. The insight of the wise who move about in the realm of imagelessness and its solitude is pure. That is, for the wise all "things" are wiped away and even the state of imagelessness ceases to exist.

Chapter V

The Mind System

THEN MAHAMATI SAID to the Blessed One: Pray tell us, Blessed One, what is meant by the mind (*citta*)?

The Blessed One replied: All things of this world, be they seemingly good or bad, faulty or faultless, effect-producing or not effect-producing, receptive or non-receptive, may be divided into two classes: evil out-flowings and the non out-flowing good. The five grasping elements that make up the aggregates of personality, namely, form, sensation, perception, discrimination, and consciousness, and that are imagined to be good and bad, have their rise in the habit-energy of the mind-system,—they are the evil out-flowings of life. The spiritual attainments and the joys of the Samadhis and the fruitage of the Samapattis that come to the wise through their self-realisation of Noble Wisdom and that culminate in their return and participation in the relations of the triple world are called the non out-flowing good.

The mind-system which is the source of the evil out-flowings consists of the five sense-organs and their accompanying sense-minds (*vijnanas*) all of which are unified in the discriminating-mind (*manovijnana*). There is an unending succession of sense-concepts flowing into this discriminating or thinking-mind which combines them and discriminates them and passes judgement upon them as to their goodness or badness. Then follows aversion to or desire for them and attachment and deed; thus the entire system moves on continuously and closely bound together. But it fails to see and understand that what it sees and discriminates and grasps is only a manifestation of its own activity and has no other basis, and so the mind goes on erroneously perceiving and discriminating differences of forms and qualities, not remaining still even for a minute.

In the mind-system there are three modes of activity distinguishable: the sense-minds functioning while remaining in their original nature, the sense-minds as producing effects, and the sense-minds as evolving. By normal functioning the sense-minds grasp appropriate elements of their external world, by which sensation and perception arise at once and by degrees in every sense-organ and every sense-mind, in the pores of the skin, and even in the atoms that make up the body, by which the whole field is apprehended like a mirror reflecting objects, and not realising that the external world itself is only a manifestation of mind. The second mode of activity produces effects by which these sensations react on the discriminating mind to produce perceptions, attractions, aversions, grasping, deed and habit. The third mode of activity has to do with the growth, development and passing of the mind-system, that is, the mind-system is in subjection to its own habit-energy accumulated from beginningless time, as for instance: the "eyeness" in the eye that predisposes it to grasp and become attached to multiple forms and appearances. In this way the activities of the evolving mind-system by reason of its habit-energy stirs up waves of objectivity on the face of Universal Mind which in turn conditions the activities and evolvement of the mind-system. Appearances, perception, attraction, grasping, deed, habit, reaction, condition one another incessantly, and the functioning sense-minds, the discriminating-mind and Universal Mind are thus bound up together. Thus, by reason of discrimination of that which by nature is maya-like and unreal false-imagination and erroneous reasoning takes place, action follows and its habit-energy accumulates thereby defiling the pure face of Universal Mind, and as a result the mind-system comes into functioning and the physical body has its genesis. But the discriminating-mind has no thought that by its discriminations and attachments it is conditioning the whole body and so the sense-minds and the discriminating-mind go on mutually related and mutually conditioned in a most intimate manner and building up a world of representations out of the activities of its own imagination. As a mirror reflects forms, the perceiving senses perceive appearances which the discriminating-mind gathers together and proceeds to discriminate, to name and become attached to. Between these two functions there is no gap, nevertheless, they are mutually conditioning. The perceiving senses grasp that for which they have an affinity, and there is a transformation takes place in their structure by reason of which the mind proceeds to combine, discriminate, apprise, and act; then follows habit-energy and the establishing of the mind and its continuance.

The discriminating-mind because of its capacity to discriminate, judge, select and reason about, is also called the thinking, or intellectual-mind. There are three divisions of its mental activity: mentation which functions in connection with attachment to objects and ideas, mentation that functions in connection with general ideas, and mentation that examines into the validity of these general ideas. The mentation which functions in connection with attachment to objects and ideas derived from discrimination, discriminates the mind from its mental processes and accepts the ideas from it as being real and becomes attached to them. A variety of false judgements are thus arrived at as to being, multiplicity, individuality, value, etc., a strong grasping takes place which is perpetuated by habit-energy and thus discrimination goes on asserting itself.

These mental processes give rise to general conceptions of warmth, fluidity, motility, and solidity, as characterising the objects of discrimination, while the tenacious holding to these general ideas gives rise to proposition, reason, definition, and illustration, all of which lead to the assertions of relative knowledge and the establishment of confidence in birth, self-nature, and an ego-soul.

By mentation as an examining function is meant the intellectual act of examining into these general conclusions as to their validity, significance, and truthfulness. This is the faculty that leads to understanding, right-knowledge and points the way to self-realisation.

THEN MAHAMATI SAID to the Blessed One: Pray tell us, Blessed One, what relation ego-personality bears to the mind-system?

The Blessed One replied: To explain it, it is first necessary to speak of the self-nature of the five grasping aggregates that make up personality, although as I have already shown they are empty, un-born, and without self-nature. These five grasping aggregates are: form, sensation, perception, discrimination, consciousness. Of these, form belongs to what is made of the so-called primary elements, whatever they may be. The four remaining aggregates are without form and ought not to be reckoned as four, because they merge imperceptibly into one another. They are like space which cannot be numbered; it is only due to imagination that they are discriminated and likened to space. Because things are endowed with appearances of being, characteristic-marks, perceivableness, abode, work, one can say that they are born of effect-producing causes, but this can not be said of these four intangible aggregates for they are without form and marks. These four mental aggregates that make up personality are beyond calculability, they are beyond the four propositions, they are not to be predicated as existing nor as not existing, but together they constitute what is known as mortal-mind. They are even more maya-like and dream-like than are things, nevertheless, as discriminating mortal-mind they obstruct the self-realisation of Noble Wisdom. But it is only by the ignorant that they are enumerated and thought of as an ego-personality; the wise do not do so. This discrimination of the five aggregates that make up personality and that serve as a basis for an ego-soul and ground for its desires and self-interests must be given up, and in its place the truth of imagelessness and solitude should be established.

THEN SAID MAHAMATI to the Blessed One: Pray tell us, Blessed One, about Universal Mind and its relation to the lower mind-system?

The Blessed One replied: The sense-minds and their centralised discriminating-mind are related to the external world which is a manifestation of itself and is given over to perceiving, discriminating, and grasping its maya-like appearances. Universal Mind (Alaya-vijnana) transcends all individuation and limits. Universal Mind is thoroughly pure in its essential nature, subsisting unchanged and free from faults of impermanence, undisturbed by egoism, unruffled by distinctions, desires and aversions. Universal Mind is like a great ocean, its surface ruffled by waves and surges but its depths remaining forever unmoved. In itself it is devoid of personality and all that belongs to it, but by reason of the defilement upon its face it is like an actor and plays a variety of parts, among which a mutual functioning takes place and the mind-system arises. The principle of intellection becomes divided and mind, the functions of mind, the evil out-flowings of mind, take on individuation. The sevenfold gradation of mind appears:

namely, intuitive self-realisation, thinking-desiring-discriminating, seeing, hearing, tasting, smelling, touching, and all their interactions and reactions take their rise.

The discriminating-mind is the cause of the sense-minds and is their support and with them is kept functioning as it describes and becomes attached to a world of objects, and then, by means of its habit-energy, it defiles the face of Universal Mind. Thus Universal Mind becomes the storage and clearing house of all the accumulated products of mentation and action since beginningless time.

Between Universal Mind and the individual discriminating-mind is the intuitive-mind (*manas*) which is dependent upon Universal Mind for its cause and support and enters into relations with both. It partakes of the universality of Universal Mind, shares its purity, and like it, is above form and momentariness. It is through the intuitive-mind that the good non out-flowings emerge, are manifested and are realised. Fortunate it is that intuition is not momentary for if the enlightenment which comes by intuition were momentary the wise would lose their "wiseness" which they do not. But the intuitive-mind enters into relations with the lower mind-system, shares its experiences and reflects upon its activities.

Intuitive-mind is one with Universal Mind by reason of its participation in Transcendental Intelligence (*Arya-jnana*), and is one with the mind-system by its comprehension of differentiated knowledge (*vijnana*). Intuitive-mind has no body of its own nor any marks by which it can be differentiated. Universal Mind is its cause and support but it is evolved along with the notion of an ego and what belongs to it, to which it clings and upon which it reflects. Through intuitive-mind, by the faculty of intuition which is a mingling of both identity and perceiving, the inconceivable wisdom of Universal Mind is revealed and made realisable. Like Universal Mind it can not be the source of error.

The discriminating-mind is a dancer and a magician with the objective world as his stage. Intuitive-mind is the wise jester who travels with the magician and reflects upon his emptiness and transiency. Universal Mind keeps the record and knows what must be and what may be. It is because of the activities of the discriminating-mind that error rises and an objective world evolves and the notion of an ego-soul becomes established. If and when the discriminating-mind can be gotten rid of, the whole mind-system will cease to function and Universal Mind will alone remain. Getting rid of the discriminating-mind removes the cause of all error.

THEN SAID MAHAMATI to the Blessed One: Pray tell us, Blessed One, what is meant by the cessation of the mind-system?

The Blessed One replied: The five sense-functions and their discriminating and thinking function have their risings and complete endings from moment to moment. They are born with discrimination as cause, with form and appearance and objectivity closely linked together as condition. The will-to-live is the mother, ignorance is the father. By setting up names and forms greed is multiplied and thus the mind goes mutually conditioning and being conditioned. By becoming attached to names and forms, not realising that they have no more basis than the activities of the mind itself, error rises, false-imagination as-to pleasure and pain rises, and the way to emancipation is blocked. The lower system of sense-minds and the discriminating-mind do not really suffer pleasure and pain-they only imagine they do. Pleasure and pain are the deceptive reactions of mortal-mind as it grasps an imaginary objective world.

There are two ways in which the ceasing of the mind-system may take place: as regards form, and as regards continuation. The sense-organs function as regards form by the interaction of form, contact and grasping; and they cease to function when this contact is broken. As regards continuation,—when these interactions of form, contact and grasping cease, there is no more continuation of the seeing, hearing and other sense functions; with the ceasing of these sense functions, the discriminations, graspings and attachments of the discriminating-mind cease; and with their ceasing act and deed and their habit-energy cease, and there is no more accumulation of karma-defilement on the face of Universal Mind.

If the evolving mortal-mind were of the same nature as Universal Mind the cessation of the lower mind-system would mean the cessation of Universal Mind, but they are different for Universal Mind is not the cause of mortal-mind. There is no cessation of Universal Mind in its pure and essence-nature. What ceases to function is not Universal Mind in its essence-nature, but is the cessation of the effect-producing defilements upon its face that have been caused by the accumulation of the habit-energy of the activities of the discriminating and thinking mortal-mind. There is no cessation of Divine Mind which, in itself, is the abode of Reality and the Womb of Truth.

By the cessation of the sense-minds is meant, not the cessation of their perceiving functions, but the cessation of their discriminating and naming activities which are centralised in the discriminating mortal-mind. By the cessation of the mind-system as a whole is meant, the cessation of discrimination, the clearing away of the various attachments, and, therefore, the clearing away of the defilements of habit-energy on the face of Universal Mind which have been accumulating since beginningless time by reason of these discriminations, attachments, erroneous reasonings, and following acts. The cessation of the continuation aspect of the mind-system as a whole, takes place when there is the cessation of that which supports the mind-system, namely, the discriminating mortal-mind. With the cessation of mortal-mind the entire world of maya and desire disappears. Getting rid of the discriminating mortal-mind is Nirvana.

But the cessation of the discriminating-mind can not take place until there has been a "turning-about" in the deepest seat of consciousness. The mental habit of looking outward by the discriminating-mind upon an external objective world must be given up, and a new habit if realising Truth within the intuitive-mind by becoming one with Truth itself must be established. Until this intuitive self-realisation of Noble Wisdom is attained, the evolving mind-system will go on. But when an insight into the five Dharmas, the three self-natures, and the twofold egolessness is attained, then the way will be opened for this "turning-about" to take place. With the ending of pleasure and pain, of conflicting ideas, of the disturbing interests of egoism, a state of tranquillisation will be attained in which the truths of emancipation will be fully understood and there will be no further evil outflowings of the mind-system to interfere with the perfect self-realisation of Noble Wisdom.

Chapter VI

Transcendental Intelligence

THEN SAID MAHAMATI: Pray tell us, Blessed One, what constitutes Transcendental Intelligence?

The Blessed One replied: Transcendental Intelligence is the inner state of self-realisation of Noble Wisdom. It is realised suddenly and intuitively as the "turning-about" takes place in the deepest seat of consciousness; it neither enters nor goes out-it is like the moon seen in water. Transcendental Intelligence is not subject to birth nor destruction; it has nothing to do with combination nor concordance; it is devoid of attachment and accumulation; it transcends all dualistic conceptions.

When Transcendental Intelligence is considered, four things must be kept in mind: words, meanings, teachings and Noble Wisdom (Arya-prajna). Words are employed to express meanings but they are dependent upon discriminations and memory as cause, and upon the employment of sounds or letters by which a mutual transference of meaning is possible. Words are only symbols and may or may not clearly and fully express the meaning intended and, moreover, words may be understood quite differently from what was intended by the speaker. Words are neither different nor not different from meaning and meaning stands in the same relation to words. If meaning is different from words it could not be made manifest by means of words; but meaning is illumined by words as things are by a lamp. Words are just like a man carrying a lamp to look for his property, by which he can say: this is my property. Just so, by means of words and speech originating in discrimination, the Bodhisattva can enter into the meaning of the teachings of the Tathagatas and through the meaning he can enter into the exalted state of self-realisation of Noble Wisdom, which, in itself, is free from word discrimination. But if a man becomes attached to the literal meaning of words and holds fast to the illusion that words and meaning are in agreement, especially in such things as Nirvana which is un-born and un-dying, or as to distinctions of the Vehicles, the five Dharmas, the three self-natures, then he will fail to understand the true meaning and will become entangled in assertions and refutations. Just as varieties of objects are seen and discriminated in dreams and in visions, so ideas and statements are discriminated erroneously and error goes on multiplying.

The ignorant and simple-minded declare that meaning is not otherwise than words, that as words are, so is meaning. They think that as meaning has no body of its own that it cannot be different from words and, therefore, declare meaning to be identical with words. In this they are ignorant of the nature of words, which are subject to birth and death, whereas meaning is not; words are dependent upon letters and meaning is not; meaning is apart from existence and non-existence, it has no substratum, it is un-born. The Tathagatas do not teach a Dharma that is dependent upon letters. Anyone who teaches a doctrine that is dependent upon letters and words is a mere prattler, because Truth is beyond letters and words and books.

This does not mean that words and books never declare what is in conformity with meaning and truth, but it means that words and books are dependent upon discriminations, while meaning and truth are not; moreover, words and books are subject to the interpretation of individual minds, while meaning and truth are not. But if Truth is not expressed in words and books, the scriptures which contain the meaning of Truth would disappear, and when the scriptures disappear there will be no more disciples and masters and Bodhisattvas and Buddhas, and there will be nothing to teach. But no one must become attached to the words of the scriptures because even the canonical texts sometimes deviate from their straightforward course owing to the imperfect functioning of sentient minds. Religious discourses are given by myself and other Tathagatas in response to the varying needs and faiths of all manner of beings, in order to free them from dependence upon the thinking function of the mind-system, but they are not given to take the place of self-realisation of Noble Wisdom. When there is recognition that there is nothing in the world but what is seen of the mind itself, all dualistic discriminations will be discarded and the truth of imagelessness will be understood, and will be seen to be in conformity with meaning rather than with words and letters.

The ignorant and simple-minded being fascinated with their self-imaginations and erroneous reasonings, keep on dancing and leaping about, but are unable to understand the discourse by words about the truth of self-realisation, much less are they able to understand the Truth itself. Clinging to the external world, they cling to the study of books which are a means only, and do not know properly how to ascertain the truth of self-realisation, which is Truth unspoiled by the four propositions. Self-realisation is an exalted state of inner attainment which transcends all dualistic thinking and which is above the mind-system with its logic, reasoning, theorising, and illustrations. The Tathagatas discourse to the ignorant, but sustain the Bodhisattvas as they seek self-realisation of Noble Wisdom.

Therefore, let every disciple take good heed not to become attached to words as being in perfect conformity with meaning, because Truth is not in the letters. When a man with his finger-tip points to something to somebody, the finger-tip may be mistaken for the thing pointed at; in like manner the ignorant and simple-minded, like children, are unable even to the day of their death to abandon the idea that in the finger-tip of words there is the meaning itself. They cannot realise Ultimate Reality because of their intent clinging to words which were intended to be no more than a pointing finger.

Words and their discrimination bind one to the dreary round of rebirths into the world of birth-and-death; meaning stands alone and is a guide to Nirvana. Meaning is attained by much learning, and much learning is attained by be coming conversant with meaning and not with words; therefore, let seekers for truth reverently approach those who are wise and avoid the sticklers for particular words.

As for teachings: there are priests and popular preachers who are given to ritual and ceremony and who are skilled in various incantations and in the art of eloquence; they should not be honored nor reverently attended upon, for what one gains from them is emotional excitement and worldly enjoyment; it is not the Dharma. Such preachers, by their clever manipulation of words and phrases and various reasonings and incantations, being the mere prattle of a child, as far as one can make out and not at all in accordance with truth nor in unison with meaning, only serves to awaken sentiment and emotion, while it stupifies the mind. As he himself does not understand the meaning of all things, he only confuses the minds of his hearers with his dualistic views. Not understanding himself, that there is nothing but what is seen of the mind, and himself attached to the notion of self-nature in external things, and unable to know one path from another, he has no deliverance to offer others. Thus these priests and popular preachers who are clever in various incantations and skilled in the art of eloquence, themselves never being emancipated from such calamities as birth, old age, disease, sorrow, lamentation, pain and despair, lead the ignorant into bewilderment by means of their various words, phrases, examples, and conclusions.

Then there are the materialistic philosophers. No respect nor service is to be shown them because their teachings, though they may be explained by using hundreds of thousands of words and phrases, do not go beyond the concerns of this world and this body and in the end they lead to suffering. As the materialists recognise no truth as existing by itself, they are split up into many schools, each of which clings to its own way of reasoning. '

But there is that which does not belong to materialism and which is not reached by the knowledge of the philosophers who cling to false-discriminations and erroneous reasonings because they fail to see that, fundamentally, there is no reality in external objects. When it is recognised that there is nothing beyond what is seen of the mind itself, the discrimination of being and non-being ceases and, as there is thus no external world as the object of perception, nothing remains but the solitude of Reality. This does not belong to the materialistic philosophers, it is the domain of the Tathagatas. If such things are imagined as the coming and going of the mind-system, vanishing and appearing, solicitation, attachment, intense affection, a philosophic hypothesis, a theory, an abode, a sense-concept; atomic attraction, organism, growth, thirst, grasping,—these things belong to materialism, they are not mine. These are things that are the object of worldly interest, to be sensed, handled and tasted; these are the things that attract one, that bind one to the external world; these are the things that appear in the elements that make up the aggregates of personality where, owing to the procreative force of lust, there arise all kinds of disaster, birth, sorrow, lamentation, pain, despair, disease, old age, death. All these things concern worldly interests and enjoyment; they lie along the path of the philosophers, which is not the path of the Dharma. When the true egolessness of things and persons is understood, discrimination ceases to assert itself; the lower mind-system ceases to function; the various Bodhisattva stages are followed one after another; the Bodhisattva is able to utter his ten inexhaustible vows and is anointed by all the Buddhas. The Bodhisattva becomes master of himself and of all things by virtue of a life of spontaneous and radiant effortlessness. Thus the Dharma, which is Transcendental Intelligence, transcends all discriminations, all false-reasonings, all philosophical systems, all dualism.

THEN MAHAMATI SAID to the Blessed One: In the Scriptures mention is made of the Womb of Tathagatahood and it is taught that that which is born of it is by nature bright and pure, originally unspotted and endowed with the thirty-two marks of excellence. As it is described it is a precious gem but wrapped in a dirty garment soiled by greed, anger, folly and false-imagination. We are taught that this Buddha-nature immanent in every one is eternal, unchanging, auspicious. Is not this which is born of the Womb of Tathagatahood the same as the soul-substance that is taught by the philosophers? The Divine Atman as taught by them is also claimed to be eternal, inscrutable, unchanging, imperishable. Is there, or is there not a difference?

The Blessed One replied: No, Mahamati, my Womb of Tathagatahood is not the same as the Divine Atman as taught by the philosophers. What I teach is Tathagatahood in the sense of Dharmakaya, Ultimate Oneness, Nirvana, emptiness, unbornness, unqualifiedness, devoid of will-effort. The reason why I teach the doctrine of Tathagatahood is to cause the ignorant and simple-minded to lay aside their fears as they listen to the teaching of egolessness and come to understand the state of non-discrimination and imagelessness. The religious teachings of the Tathagatas are just like a potter making various vessels by his own skill of hand with the aid of rod, water and thread, out of the one mass of clay, so the Tathagatas by their command of skillful means issuing from Noble Wisdom, by various terms, expressions, and symbols, preach the twofold egolessness in order to remove the last trace of discrimination that is preventing disciples from attaining a self-realisation of Noble Wisdom. The doctrine of the Tathagata-womb is disclosed in order to awaken philosophers from their clinging to the notion of a Divine Atman as transcendental personality, so that their minds that have become attached to the imaginary notion of "soul" as being something self-existent, may be quickly awakened to a state of perfect enlightenment.

All such notions as causation, succession, atoms, primary elements, that make up personality, personal soul, Supreme Spirit, Sovereign God, Creator, are all figments of the imagination and manifestations of mind. No, Mahamati, the Tathagata*'s doctrine of the Womb of Tathagatahood is not the same as the philosopher's Atman.

The Bodhisattva is said to have well grasped the teachings of the Tathagatas when, all alone in a lonely place, by means of his Transcendental Intelligence, he walks the path leading to Nirvana. Thereon his mind will unfold by perceiving, thinking, meditating, and, abiding in the practise of concentration until he attains the "turning about" at the source of habit-energy, he will thereafter lead a life of excellent deeds. His mind concentrated on the state of Buddhahood, he will become thoroughly conversant with the noble truth of self-realisation; he will become perfect master of his own mind; he will be like a gem radiating many colors; he will be able to assume bodies of transformation; he will be able to enter into the minds of all to help them; and, finally, by gradually ascending the stages he will become established in the perfect Transcendental Intelligence of the Tathagatas.

Nevertheless, Transcendental Intelligence (*Arya-jnana*) is not Noble Wisdom (*Arya-prajna*) itself; it is only an intuitive awareness of it. Noble Wisdom is a perfect state of imagelessness; it is the Womb of "Suchness"; it is the all-conserving Divine Mind (*Alaya-vijnana*) which in its pure Essence forever abides in perfect patience and undisturbed tranquility.

Chapter VII

Self-Realisation

THEN SAID MAHAMATI: Pray tell us, Blessed One, what is the nature of self-realisation by reason of which we shall be able to attain Transcendental Intelligence?

The Blessed One replied: Transcendental Intelligence rises when the intellectual-mind reaches its limit and, if things are to be realised in their true and essence nature, its processes of mentation, which are based on particularised ideas, discriminations and judgments, must be transcended by an appeal to some higher faculty of cognition, if there be such a higher faculty. There is such a faculty in the intuitive-mind (Manas), which as we have seen is the link between the intellectual-mind and Universal Mind. While it is not an individualised organ like the intellectual-mind, it has that which is much better,—direct dependence upon Universal Mind. While intuition does not give information that can be analysed and discriminated, it gives that which is far superior,—self-realisation through identification.

MAHAMATI THEN ASKED the Blessed One, saying: Pray tell us, Blessed One, what clear understandings an earnest disciple should have if he is to be successful in the discipline that leads to self-realisation?

The Blessed One replied: There are four things by the fulfilling of which an earnest disciple may gain self-realisation of Noble Wisdom and become a Bodhisattva-Mahasattva: First, he must have a clear understanding that all things are only manifestations of the mind itself; second, he must discard the notion of birth, abiding and disappearance; third, he must clearly understand the egolessness of both things and persons; and fourth, he must have a true conception of what constitutes self-realisation of Noble Wisdom. Provided with these four understandings, earnest disciples may become Bodhisattvas and attain Transcendental Intelligence.

As to the first; he must recognise and be fully convinced that this triple world is nothing but a complex manifestation of one's mental activities; that it is devoid of selfness and its belongings; that there are no strivings, no comings, no goings. He must recognise and accept the fact that this triple world is manifested and imagined as real only under the influence of habit-energy that has been accumulated since the beginning less past by reason of memory, false-imagination, false-reasoning, and attachments to the multiplicities of objects and reactions in close relationship and in conformity to ideas of body-property-and-abode.

As to the second; he must recognise and be convinced that all things are to be regarded as forms seen in a vision and a dream, empty of substance, un-born and without self-nature; that all things exist only by reason of a complicated network of causation which owes its rise to discrimination and attachment and which eventuates in the rise of the mind-system and its belongings and evolvements.

As to the third; he must recognise and patiently accept the fact that his own mind and personality is also mind-constructed, that it is empty of substance, unborn and egoless. With these three things clearly in mind, the Bodhisattva will be able to enter into the truth of imagelessness.

As to the fourth; he must have a true conception of what constitutes self-realisation of Noble Wisdom. First, it is not comparable to the perceptions attained by the sense-mind, neither is it comparable to the cognition of the discriminating and intellectual-mind. Both of these presuppose a difference between self and not-self and the knowledge so attained is characterised by individuality and generality. Self-realisation is based on identity and oneness; there is nothing to be discriminated nor predicated concerning it. But to enter into it the Bodhisattva must be free from all presuppositions and attachments to things, ideas and selfness.

THEN SAID MAHAMATI to the Blessed One: Pray tell us, Blessed One, concerning the characteristics of deep attachments to existence and as to how we may become detached from existence?

The Blessed One replied: When one tries to understand the significance of things by means of words and discriminations, there follow immeasurably deep-seated attachments to existence. For instance, there are the deep-seated attachments to signs of individuality, to causation, to the notion of being and non-being, to the discrimination of birth and death, of doing and not-doing, to the habit of discrimination itself upon which the philosophers are so dependent.

There are three attachments that are especially deep-seated in the minds of all; greed, anger and infatuation, which are based on lust, fear and pride. Back of these lies discrimination and desire which is procreative and is accompanied with excitement and avariciousness and love of comfort and desire for eternal life; and, following, is a succession of rebirths on the five paths of existence and a continuation of attachments. But if these attachments are broken off, no signs of attachment nor of detachment will remain because they are based on things that are non-existent; when this truth is clearly understood the net of attachment is cleared away.

But depending upon and attaching itself to the triple combination which works in unison there is the rising and the continuation of the mind-system incessantly functioning, and because of it there is the deeply-felt and continuous assertion of the will-to-live. When the triple combination that causes the functioning of the mind-system ceases to exist, there is the triple emancipation and there is no further rising of any combination. When the existence and the non-existence of the external world are recognised as rising from the mind itself, then the Bodhisattva is prepared to enter into the state of imagelessness and therein to see into the emptiness which characterises all discrimination and all the deep-seated attachments resulting therefrom. Therein he will see no signs of deep-rooted attachment nor detachment; therein he will see no one in bondage and no one in emancipation, except those who themselves cherish bondage and emancipation, because in all things there is no "substance" to be taken hold of.

But so long as these discriminations are cherished by the ignorant and simple-minded they go on attaching themselves to them and, like the silkworm, go on spinning their thread of discrimination and enwrapping themselves and others, and are charmed with their prison. But to the wise there are no signs of attachment nor of detachment; all things are seen as abiding in solitude where there is no evolving of discrimination. Mahamati, you and all the Bodhisattvas should have your abode where you can see all things from the view-point of solitude.

Mahamati, when you and other Bodhisattvas understand well the distinction between attachment and detachment, you will be in possession of skillful means for avoiding becoming attached to words according to which one proceeds to grasp meanings. Free from the domination of words you will be able to establish yourselves where there will be a "turning about" in the deepest seat of consciousness by means of which you will attain self-realisation of Noble Wisdom and be able to enter into all the Buddha-lands and assemblies. There you will be stamped with the stamp of the powers, self-command, the psychic faculties, and will be endowed with the wisdom and the power of the ten inexhaustible vows, and will become radiant with the variegated rays of the Transformation Bodies. Therewith you will shine without effort like the moon, the sun, the magic wishing-jewel, and at every stage will view things as being of perfect oneness with yourself, uncontaminated by any self-consciousness. Seeing that all things are like a dream, you will be able to enter into the stage of the Tathagatas and be able to deliver discourses on the Dharma to the world of beings in accordance with their needs and be able to free them from all dualistic notions and false discriminations.

Mahamati, there are two ways of considering self-realisation: namely, the teachings about it, and the realisation itself. The teachings as variously given in the nine divisions of the doctrinal works, for the instructions of those who are inclined toward it, by making use of skillful means and expedients, are intended to awaken in all beings a true perception of the Dharma. The teachings are designed to keep one away from all the dualistic notions of being and non-being and oneness and otherness.

Realisation itself is within the inner consciousness. It is an inner experience that has no connection with the lower mind-system and its discriminations of words, ideas and philosophical speculations. It shines out with its own clear light to reveal the error and foolishness of mind-constructed teachings, to render impotent evil influences from without, and to guide one unerringly to the realm of the good non-outflowings. Mahamati, when the earnest disciple and Bodhisattva is provided with these requirements, the way is open to his perfect attainment of self-realisation of Noble Wisdom, and to the full enjoyment of the fruits that arise there from.

THEN MAHAMATI ASKED the Blessed One, saying: Pray tell us, Blessed One, about the One Vehicle which the Blessed One has said characterises the attainment of the inner self-realisation of Noble Wisdom?

The Blessed One replied: In order to discard more easily discriminations and erroneous reasonings, the Bodhisattva should retire by himself to a quiet, secluded place where he may reflect within himself without relying on anyone else, and there let him exert himself to make successive advances along the stages; this solitude is the characteristic feature of the inner attainment of self-realisation of Noble Wisdom.

I call this the One Vehicle, not because it is the One Vehicle, but because it is only in solitude that one is able to recognise and realise the path of the One Vehicle. So long as the mind is distracted and is making conscious effort, there can be no culmination as regards the various vehicles; it is only when the mind is alone and quiet that it is able to forsake the discriminations of the external world and seek realisation of an inner realm where there is neither vehicle nor one who rides in it. I speak of the three vehicles in order to carry the ignorant. I do not speak much about the One Vehicle because there is no way by which earnest disciples and masters can realise Nirvana, unaided. According to the discourses of the Tathagatas earnest disciples should be segregated and disciplined and trained in meditation and dhyana whereby they are aided by many devices and expedients to realise emancipation. It is because earnest disciples and masters have not fully destroyed the habit-energy of karma and the hindrances of discriminative knowledge and human passion that they are often unable to accept the twofold egolessness and the inconceivable transformation death, that I preach the triple vehicle and not the One Vehicle. When earnest disciples have gotten rid of all their evil habit-energy and been able to realise the twofold egolessness, then they will not be intoxicated by the bliss of the Samadhis and will be awakened into the super-realm of the good non-outflowings. Being awakened into the realm of the good non-outflowings, they will be able to gather up all the requisites for the attainment of Noble Wisdom which is beyond conception and is of sovereign power. But really, Mahamati, there are no vehicles, and so I speak of the One Vehicle. Mahamati, the full recognition of the One Vehicle has never been attained by either earnest disciples, masters, or even by the great Brahma; it has been attained only by the Tathagatas themselves. That is the reason that it is known as the One Vehicle. I do not, speak much about it because there is no way by which earnest disciples can realise Nirvana unaided.

THEN MAHAMATI ASKED the Blessed One, saying: What are the steps that will lead an awakened disciple toward the self-realisation of Noble Wisdom?

The Blessed One replied: The beginning lies in the recognition that the external world is only a manifestation of the activities of the mind itself, and that the mind grasps it as an external world simply because of its habit of discrimination and false-reasoning. The disciple must get into the habit of looking at things truthfully. He must recognise the fact that the world has no self-nature, that it is un-born, that it is like a passing cloud, like an imaginary wheel made by a revolving firebrand, like the castle of the Gandharvas, like the moon reflected in the ocean, like a vision, a mirage, a dream. He must come to understand that mind in its essence-nature has nothing to do with discrimination nor causation; he must not listen to discourses based on the imaginary terms of qualifications; he must understand that Universal Mind in its pure essence is a state of imagelessness, that it is only because of the accumulated defilements on its face that body-property-and-abode appear to be its manifestations, that in its own pure nature it is unaffected and unaffecting by such changes as rising, abiding and destruction; he must fully understand that all these things come with the awakening of the notion of an ego-soul and its conscious mind. Therefore, Mahamati, let those disciples who wish to realise Noble Wisdom by following the Tathagata Vehicle desist from all discrimination and erroneous reasoning about such notions as the elements that make up the aggregates of personality and its sense-world or about such ideas as causation, rising, abiding and destruction, and exercise themselves in the discipline of dhyana that leads to the realisation of Noble Wisdom.

To practice dhyana, the earnest disciple should retire to a quiet and solitary place, remembering that life-long habits of discriminative thinking cannot be broken off easily nor quickly. There are four kinds of concentrative meditation (dhyana): The dhyana practised by the ignorant; the dhyana devoted to the examination of meaning; the dhyana with "suchness" (tathata) for its object; and the dhyana of the Tathagatas.

The dhyana practised by the ignorant is the one resorted to by those who are following the example of the disciples and masters but who do not understand its purpose and, therefore, it becomes "still-sitting" with vacant minds. This dhyana is practised, also, by those who, despising the body, see it as a shadow and a skeleton full of suffering and impurity, and yet who cling to the notion of an ego, seek to attain emancipation by the mere cessation of thought.

The dhyana devoted to the examination of meaning, is the one practised by those who, perceiving the untenability of such ideas as self, other and both, which are held by the philosophers, and who have passed beyond the twofold-egolessness, devote dhyana to an examination of the significance of egolessness and the' differentiations of the Bodhisattva stages.

The dhyana with Tathata, or "Suchness," or Oneness, or the Divine Name, for its object is practised by those earnest disciples and masters who, while fully recognising the twofold egolessness and the imagelessness of Tathata, yet cling to the notion of an ultimate Tathata.

The dhyana of the Tathagatas is the dhyana of those who are entering upon the stage of Tathagatahood and who, abiding in the triple bliss which characterises the self-realisation of Noble Wisdom, are devoting themselves for the sake of all beings to the accomplishment of incomprehensible works for their emancipation. This is the pure dhyana of the Tathagatas. When all lesser things and ideas are transcended and forgotten, and there remains only a perfect state of imagelessness where Tathagata and Tathata are merged into perfect Oneness, then the Buddhas will come together from all their Buddha-lands and with shining hands resting on his forehead will welcome a new Tathagata.

Chapter VIII

The Attainment of Self- Realisation

THEN SAID MAHAMATI to the Blessed One: Pray tell us more as to what constitutes the state of self-realisation?

The Blessed One replied: In the life of an earnest disciple there are two aspects that are to be distinguished: namely, the state of attachment to the self-natures arising from discrimination of himself and his field of consciousness to which he is related; and second, the excellent and exalted state of self-realisation of Noble Wisdom. The state of attachment to the discriminations of the self-natures of things, ideas and selfhood is accompanied by emotions of pleasure or aversion according to experience or as laid down in books of logic. Conforming himself to the egolessness of things and holding back wrong views as to his own egoness, he should abandon these thoughts and hold himself firmly to the continuously ascending journey of the stages.

The exalted state of self-realisation as it relates to an earnest disciple is a state of mental concentration in which he seeks to identify himself with Noble Wisdom. In that effort he must seek to annihilate all vagrant thoughts and notions belonging to the externality of things, and all ideas of individuality and generality, of suffering and impermanence, and cultivate the noblest ideas of egolessness and emptiness and imagelessness; thus will he attain a realisation of truth that is free from passion and is ever serene. When this active effort at mental concentration is successful it is followed by a more passive, receptive state of Samadhi in which the earnest disciple will enter into the blissful abode of Noble Wisdom and experience its consummations in the transformations of Samapatti. This is an earnest disciple's first experience of the exalted state of realisation, but as yet there is no discarding of habit-energy nor escaping from the transformation of death.

Having attained this exalted and blissful state of realisation as far as it can be attained by disciples, the Bodhisattva must not give himself up to the enjoyment of its bliss, for that would mean cessation, but should think compassionately of other beings and keep ever fresh his original vows; he should never let himself rest in nor exert himself in the bliss of the Samadhis.

But, Mahamati, as earnest disciples go on trying to advance on the path that leads to full realisation, there is one danger against which they must be on their guard. Disciples may not appreciate that the mind-system, because of its accumulated habit-energy, goes on functioning, more or less unconsciously, as long as they live. They may sometimes think that they can expedite the attainment of their goal of tranquillisation by entirely suppressing the activities of the mind-system. This is a mistake, for even if the activities of the mind are suppressed, the mind will still go on functioning because the seeds of habit-energy will still remain in it. What they think is extinction of mind, is really the non-functioning of the mind's external world to which they are no longer attached. That is, the goal of tranquillisation is to be reached not by suppressing all mind activity but by getting rid of discriminations and attachments.

Then there are others who, afraid of the suffering incident to the discriminations of life and death, unwisely seek Nirvana. They have come to see that all things subject to discrimination have no reality and so imagine that Nirvana must consist in the annihilation of the senses and their fields of sensation; they do not appreciate that birth-and-death and Nirvana are not separate one from the other. They do not know that Nirvana is Universal Mind in its purity. Therefore, these stupid ones who cling to the notion that Nirvana is a world by itself that is outside what is seen by the mind, ignoring all the teachings of the Tathagatas concerning the external world, go on rolling themselves along the wheel of birth-and-death. But when they experience the "turning-about" in their deepest consciousness which will bring with it the perfect self-realisation of Noble Wisdom, then they will understand.

The true functioning of the mind is very subtle and difficult to be understood by young disciples, even masters with all their powers of right-knowledge and Samadhis often find it baffling. It is only the Tathagatas and the Bodhisattvas who are firmly established on the seventh stage who can fully understand its workings. Those earnest disciples and masters who wish to fully understand all the aspects of the different stages of Bodhisattvahood by the aid of their right-knowledge must do so by becoming thoroughly convinced that objects of discrimination are only seen to be so by the mind and, thus, by keeping themselves away from all discriminations and false reasonings which are also of the mind itself, by ever seeking to see things truly (yathabhutam), and by planting roots of goodness in Buddha-lands that know no limits made by differentiations.

To do all this the Bodhisattva should keep himself away from all turmoil, social excitements and sleepiness; let him keep away from the treatises and writings of worldly philosophers, and from the ritual and ceremonies of professional priestcraft. Let him retire to a secluded place in the forest and there devote himself to the practise of the various spiritual disciplines, because it is only by so doing that he will become capable of attaining in this world of multiplicities a true insight into the workings of Universal Mind in its Essence. There surrounded by his good friends the Buddhas, earnest disciples will become capable of understanding the significance of the mind-system and its place as a mediating agent between the external world and

Universal Mind and he will become capable of crossing the ocean of birth-and-death which rises from ignorance, desire and deed.

Having gained a thorough understanding of the mind-system, the three self-natures, the twofold egolessness, and established himself in the measure of self-realisation that goes with that attainment, all of which may be gained by his right-knowledge, the way will be clear for the Bodhisattva's further advance along the stages of Bodhisattvahood. The disciple should then abandon the understanding of mind which he has gained by right-knowledge, which in comparison with Noble Wisdom is like a lame donkey, and entering on the eighth stage of Bodhisattvahood, he should then discipline himself in Noble Wisdom according to its three aspects.

These aspects are: First, imagelessness which comes forth when all things belonging to discipleship, mastership, and philosophy are thoroughly mastered. Second, the power added by all the Buddhas by reason of their original vows including the identification of their lives and the sharing of their merit with all sentient lives. Third, the perfect self-realisation that thus far has only been realised in a measure. As the Bodhisattva succeeds in detaching himself from viewing all things, including his own imagined egoness, in their phenomenality, and realises the states of Samadhi and Samapatti whereby he surveys the world as a vision and a dream, and being sustained by all the Buddhas, he will be able to pass on to the full attainment of the Tathagata stage, which is Noble Wisdom itself. This is the triplicity of the noble life and being furnished with this triplicity the perfect self-realisation of Noble Wisdom has been attained.

THEN MAHAMATI ASKED the Blessed One, saying: Blessed One, is the purification of the evil outflowings of the mind which come from clinging to the notions of an objective world and an empirical soul, gradual or instantaneous?

The Blessed One replied: There are three characteristic out-flows of the mind, namely, the evil outflowings that rise from thirst, grasping and attachment; the evil out-flowings that arise from the illusions of the mind and the infatuations of egoism; and the good non-outflowings that arise from Noble Wisdom. The evil out-flowings that take place from recognising an external world, which in truth is only a manifestation of mind, and from becoming attached to it, are gradually purified and not instantaneously. Good behavior can only come by the path of restraint and effort. It is like a potter making pots that is done gradually and with attention and effort. It is like the mastery of comedy, dancing, singing, lute-playing, writing, and any other art; it must be acquired gradually and laboriously. Its reward will be a clearing insight into the emptiness and transiency of all things.

The evil out-flowings that arise from the illusions of the mind and the infatuations of egoism, concern the mental life more directly and are such things as fear, anger, hatred and pride; these are purified by study and meditation and that, too, must be attained gradually and not instantaneously.

It is like the amra fruit that ripens slowly; it is like grass, shrubs, herbs and trees that grow up from the earth gradually. Each must follow the path of study and meditation by himself gradually and with effort, but because of the original vows of the Bodhisattvas and all the Tathagatas who have devoted their merits and identified their lives with all animate life that all may be emancipated, they are not without aid and encouragement; but even with the aid of the Tathagatas, the purification of the evil out-flowings of the mind are at best slow and gradual, requiring both zeal and patience. Its reward is the gradual understanding of the twofold egolessness and its patient acceptance, and the feet well set on the stages of Bodhisattvahood.

But the good non-outflowings that come with self-realisation of Noble Wisdom, is a purification that comes instantaneously by the grace of the Tathagatas. It is like a mirror reflecting all forms and images instantaneously and without discrimination; it is like the sun or the moon revealing all forms instantaneously and illuminating them dispassionately with its light. In the same way the Tathagatas lead earnest disciples to a state of imagelessness; all the accumulations of habit-energy and karma that had been collecting since beginningless time because of attachment to erroneous views which have been entertained regarding an ego-soul and its external world, are cleared away, revealing instantaneously the realm of Transcendental Intelligence that belongs to Buddhahood. Just as Universal Mind defiled by accumulations of habit-energy and karma reveals multiplicities of ego-souls and their external worlds of false-imagination, so Universal Mind cleared of its defilements through the gradual purifications of the evil out-flowings that come by effort, study and meditation, and by the gradual self-realisation of Noble Wisdom, at the long last, like the Dharmata Buddha shining forth spontaneously with the rays that issue from its pure Self-nature, shines forth instantaneously. By it the mentality of all Bodhisattvas is matured instantaneously: they find themselves in the palatial abodes of the Akanistha heavens, themselves spontaneously radiating the various treasures of its spiritual abundance.

Chapter IX
The Fruits of Self- Realisation

MAHAMATI ASKED the Blessed One: Pray tell us, Blessed One, what is the fruitage that comes with self -realisation of Noble Wisdom?

The Blessed One replied: First, there will come a clearing insight into the meaning and significance of things and following that will come an unfolding insight into the significance of the spiritual ideals (*Paramitas*) by reason of which the Bodhisattvas will be able to enter more deeply into the abode of imagelessness and be able to experience the higher Samadhis and gradually to pass through the higher stages of Bodhisattvahood.

After experiencing the "turning-about" in the deepest seat of consciousness, they will experience other Samadhis even to the highest, the Vajravimbopama, which belongs to the Tathagatas and their transformations. They will be able to enter into the realm of consciousness that lies beyond the consciousness of the mind-system, even the consciousness of Tathagatahood. They will become endowed with all the powers, psychic faculties, self-mastery, loving compassion, skillful means, and ability to enter into other Buddha-lands. Before they had attained self-realisation of Noble Wisdom they had been influenced by the self-interests of egoism, but after they attain self-realisation they will find themselves reacting spontaneously to the impulses of a great and compassionate heart endowed with skillful and boundless means and sincerely and wholly devoted to the emancipation of all beings.

MAHAMATI SAID: Blessed One, tell us about the sustaining power of the Tathagatas by which the Bodhisattvas are aided to attain self-realisation of Noble Wisdom?

The Blessed One replied: There are two kinds of sustaining power, which issue from the Tathagatas and are at the service of the Bodhisattvas, sustained by which the Bodhisattvas should prostrate themselves before them and show their appreciation by asking questions. The first kind of sustaining power is the Bodhisattva's own adoration and faith in the Buddhas by reason of which the Buddhas are able to manifest themselves and render their aid and to ordain them with their own hands. The second kind of sustaining power is the power radiating from the Tathagatas that enables the Bodhisattvas to attain and to pass through the various Samadhis and Samapattis without becoming intoxicated by their bliss.

Being sustained by the power of the Buddhas, the Bodhisattva even at the first stage will be able to attain the Samadhi known as the Light of Mahayana. in that Samadhi Bodhisattvas will become conscious of the presence of the Tathagatas coming from all their different abodes in the ten quarters to impart to the Bodhisattvas their sustaining power in various ways. As the

Bodhisattva Vajragarbha was sustained in his Samadhis and as many other Bodhisattvas of like degree and virtue have been sustained, so all earnest disciples and masters and Bodhisattvas may experience this sustaining power of the Buddhas in their Samadhis and Samapattis. The disciple's faith and the Tathagata's merit are two aspects of the same sustaining power and by it alone are the Bodhisattvas enabled to become one with the company of the Buddhas.

Whatever Samadhis, psychic faculties and teachings are realised by the Bodhisattvas, they are made possible only by the sustaining power of the Buddhas; if it were otherwise, the ignorant and the simpleminded might attain the same fruitage. Wherever the Tathagatas enter with their sustaining power there will be music, not only music made by human lips and played by human hands on various instruments, but there will be music among the grass and shrubs and trees, and in mountains and towns and palaces and hovels; much more will there be music in the hearts of those endowed with sentiency. The deaf, dumb and blind will be cured of their deficiencies and will rejoice in their emancipation. Such is the extraordinary virtue of the sustaining power imparted by the Tathagatas.

By the bestowal of this sustaining power, the Bodhisattvas are enabled to avoid the evils of passion, hatred and enslaving karma; they are enabled to transcend the dhyana of the beginners and to advance beyond the experience and truth already attained; they are enabled to demonstrate the Paramitas; and finally, to attain the stage of Tathagatahood. Mahamati, if it were not for this sustaining power, they would relapse into the ways and thoughts of the philosophers, easygoing disciples and the evil-minded, and would thus fall short of the highest attainment. For these reasons, earnest disciples and sincere Bodhisattvas are sustained by the power of all the Tathagatas.

THEN SAID MAHAMATI: It has been said by the Blessed One that by fulfilling the six Paramitas, Buddhahood is realised. Pray tell us what the Paramitas are, and how they are to be fulfilled?

The Blessed One replied: The Paramitas are ideals of spiritual perfection that are to be the guide of the Bodhisattvas on the path to self-realisation. There are six of them but they are to be considered in three different ways according to the progress of the Bodhisattva on the stages. At first they are to be considered as ideals for the worldly life; next as ideals for the mental life; and, lastly, as ideals of the spiritual and unitive life.

In the worldly life where one is still holding tenaciously to the notions of an ego-soul and what concerns it and holding fast to discriminations of dualism, if only for worldly benefits, one should cherish ideals of charity, good behavior, patience, zeal, thoughtfulness and wisdom. Even in the worldly life the practice of these virtues will bring rewards of happiness and success.

Much more in the mind-world of earnest disciples and masters will their practice bring joys of emancipation, enlightenment and peace of mind, because the Paramitas are grounded on right-knowledge and lead to thoughts of Nirvana, even if the Nirvana of their thoughts is for themselves. In the mind-world the Paramitas become more ideal and more sympathetic; charity can no longer be expressed in the giving of impersonal gifts but will call for the more costly gifts of sympathy and understanding; good behavior will call for something more than outward conformity to the five precepts because in the light of the Paramitas they must practise humility, simplicity, restraint and self-giving. Patience will call for something more than forbearance with external circumstances and the temperaments of other people: it will now call for patience with one's self. Zeal will call for something more than industry and outward show of earnestness: it will call for more self-control in the task of following the Noble Path and in manifestating the Dharma in one's own life. Thoughtfulness will give way to mindfulness wherein discriminated meanings and logical deductions and rationalisations will give way to intuitions of significance and spirit. The Paramita of Wisdom (Prajna) will no longer be concerned with pragmatic wisdom and erudition, but will reveal itself in its true perfectness of All-inclusive Truth which is Love.

The third aspect of the Paramitas as seen in the ideal perfections of the Tathagatas can only be fully understood by the Bodhisattva-Mahasattvas who are devoted to the highest spiritual discipline and have fully understood that there is nothing to be seen in the world but that which issues from the mind itself; in whose minds the discriminations of dualities has ceased to function; and seizing and clinging has become non-existent. Thus free from all attachments to individual objects and ideas, their minds are free to consider ways of benefitting and giving happiness to others, even to all sentient beings To the Bodhisattva-Mahasattvas the ideal of charity is shown in the self-yielding of the Tathagata's hope of Nirvana that all may enjoy it together. While having relations with an objective world there is no rising in the minds of the Tathagatas of discriminations between the interests of self and the interests of others, between good and evil,—there is just the spontaneity and effortless actuality of perfect behavior. To practise patience with full knowledge of this and that, of grasp and grasping, but with no thought of discrimination nor of attachment,—that is the Tathagatas Paramita of Patience. To exert oneself with energy from the first part of the night to its end in conformity with the disciplinary measures with no rising of discrimination as to comfort or discomfort,—that is the Tathagata's Paramita of Zeal. Not to discriminate between self and others in thoughts of Nirvana, but to keep the mind fixed on Nirvana,—that is the Paramita of Mindfulness. As to the Prajna-Paramita, which is Noble Wisdom, who can predicate it? When in Samadhi the mind ceases to discriminate and there is only perfect and love-filled imagelessness, then an inscrutable "turning-about" will take place in the inmost consciousness and one will have attained self-realisation of Noble Wisdom,—that is the highest Prajna-Paramita.

THEN MAHAMATI SAID to the Blessed One: You have spoken of an astral-body, a "mind-vision-body" (*manomayakaya*) which the Bodhisattvas are able to assume, as being one of the fruits of self-realisation of Noble Wisdom: pray tell us, Blessed One, what is meant by such a transcendental body?

The Blessed One replied: There are three kinds of such transcendental bodies: First, there is the one in which the Bodhisattva attains enjoyment of the Samadhis and Samapattis. Second, there is the one which is assumed by the Tathagatas according to the class of beings to be sustained, and which achieves and perfects spontaneously with no attachment and no effort. Third, there is the one in which the Tathagatas receive their intuition of Dharmakaya.

The transcendental personality that enters into the enjoyment of the Samadhis comes with the third, fourth and fifth stages as the mentations of the mindsystem become quieted and waves of consciousness are no more stirred on the face of Universal Mind. In this state, the conscious-mind is still aware, in a measure, of the bliss being experienced by this cessation of the mind's activities.

The second kind of transcendental personality is the kind assumed by the Bodhisattvas and Tathagatas as bodies of transformation by which they demonstrate their original vows in the work of achieving and perfecting; it comes with the eighth stage of Bodhisattvahood. When the Bodhisattva has a thorough-going penetration into the maya-like nature of things and understands the dharma of imagelessness, he will experience the "turning-about" in his deepest consciousness and will become able to experience the higher Samadhis even to the highest. By entering into these exalted Samadhis he attains a personality that transcends the conscious-mind, by reason of which he obtains supernatural powers of self-mastery and activities because of which he is able to move as he wishes, as quickly as a dream changes, as quickly as an image changes in a mirror. This transcendental body is not a product of the elements and yet there is something in it that is analogous to what is so produced; it is furnished with all the differences appertaining to the world of form but without their limitations; possessed of this "mind-vision-body" he is able to be present in all the assemblages in all the Buddha-lands. Just as his thoughts move instantly and without hindrance over walls and rivers and trees and mountains, and just as in memory he recalls and visits the scenes of his past experiences, so, while his mind keeps functioning in the body, his thoughts May be a hundred thousand yojanas away. In the same fashion the transcendental personality that experiences the Samadhi Vajravimbopama will be endowed with supernatural powers and psychic faculties and self-mastery by reason of which he will be able to follow the noble paths that lead to the assemblages of the Buddhas, moving about as freely as he may wish. But his wishes will no longer be self-centered nor tainted by discrimination and attachment, for this transcendental personality is not his old body, but is the transcendental embodiment of his original vows of self-yielding in order to bring all beings to maturity.

The third kind of transcendental personality is so ineffable that it is able to attain intuitions of the Dharmakaya, that is, it attains intuitions of the boundless and inscrutable cognition of Universal Mind. As Bodhisattva-Mahasattvas attain the highest of the stages and become conversant with all the treasures to be realised in Noble Wisdom, they will attain this inconceivable transformation-body which is the true nature of all the Tathagatas past, present and future, and will participate in the blissful peace which pervades the Dharma of all the Buddhas.

Chapter X

Discipleship: Lineage of the Arhats

THEN MAHAMATI ASKED the Blessed One: Pray tell us how many kinds of disciples there are?

The Blessed One replied: There are as many kinds of disciples as there are individuals, but for convenience they may be divided into two groups: disciples of the lineage of the Arhats, and disciples known as Bodhisattvas. Disciples of the lineage of the Arhats may be considered under two aspects: First, according to the number of times they will return to this life of birth-and-death; and second, according to their spiritual progress. Under the first aspect, they may be subdivided into three groups: The "Stream-entered," the "Once-returning," and the "Never-returning."

The Stream-entered are those disciples, who having freed themselves from the attachments to the lower discriminations and who have cleansed themselves from the twofold hindrances and who clearly understand the meaning of the twofold egolessness, yet who still cling to the notions of individuality and generality and to their own egoness. They will advance along the stages to the sixth only to succumb to the entrancing bliss of the Samadhis. They will be reborn seven times, or five times, or three times, before they will be able to pass the sixth stage. The Once-returning are the Arhats, and the Never-returning are the Bodhisattvas who have reached the seventh stage.

The reason for these gradations is because of their attachment to the three degrees of false-imagination: namely, faith in moral practices, doubt, and the view of their individual personality. When these three hindrances are overcome, they will be able to attain the higher stages. As to moral practices: the ignorant, simple-minded disciples obey the rules of morality, piety and penance, because they desire thereby to gain worldly advancement and happiness, with the added hope of being reborn in more favorable conditions. The Stream-entered ones do not cling to moral practices for any hope of reward for their minds are fixed on the exalted state of self-realisation; the reason they devote themselves to the details of morality is that they wish to master such truths as are in conformity with the undefiled out-flowings. As regards the hindrance of doubt in the Buddha's teachings, that will continue so long as any of the notions of discriminations are cherished and will disappear when they disappear. Attachment to the view of individual personality will be gotten rid of as the disciple gains a more thorough understanding of the notions of being and non-being, self-nature and egolessness, thereby getting rid of the attachments to his own selfness that goes with those discriminations. By breaking up and clearing away these three hindrances the Stream-entered ones will be able to discard all greed, anger and folly.

As for the Once-returning Arhats; there was once in them the discrimination of forms, signs, and appearances, but as they gradually learned by right knowledge not to view individual objects under the aspect of quality and qualifying, and as they became acquainted with what marks the attainment of the practice of dhyana, they have reached a stage of enlightenment where in one more rebirth they will be able to put an end to the clinging to their own self-interests. Free of this burden of error and its attachments, the passions will no more assert themselves and the hindrances will be cleared away forever.

Under the second aspect disciples may be grouped according to the spiritual progress they have attained, into four classes, namely, disciples (*sravaka*), masters (*pratyekabuddha*), Arhats, and Bodhisattvas.

The first class of disciples mean well but they find it difficult to understand unfamiliar ideas. Their minds are joyful when studying about and practising the things belonging to appearances that can be discriminated, but they become confused by the notion of an uninterrupted chain of causation, and they become fearful when they consider the aggregates that make up personality and its object world as being maya-like, empty and egoless. They are able to advance to the fifth or sixth stage where they are able to do away with the rising of passions, but not with the notions that give rise to passion and, therefore, they are unable to get rid of the clinging to an ego-soul and its accompanying attachments, habits and habit-energy. In this same class of disciples are the earnest disciples of other faiths, who clinging to the notions of such things as, the soul as an eternal entity, Supreme Atman, Personal God, seek a Nirvana that is in harmony with them. There are others, more materialistic in their ideas, who think that all things exist in dependence upon causation and, therefore, that Nirvana must be in like dependence. But none of these, earnest though they be, have gained an insight into the truth of the twofold egolessness and are, therefore, of limited spiritual insight as regards deliverance and non-deliverance; for them there is no emancipation. They have great self-confidence but they can never gain a true knowledge of Nirvana until they have learned to discipline themselves in the patient acceptance of the twofold egolessness.

The second class of masters are those who have gained a high degree of intellectual understanding of the truths concerning the aggregates that make up personality and its external world but who are filled with fear when they face the significance and consequences of these truths, and the demands which their learning makes upon them, that is, not to become attached to the external world and its manifold forms making for comfort and power, and to keep away from the entanglements of its social relations. They are attracted by the possibilities that are attainable by so doing, namely, the possession of miraculous powers such as dividing the personality and appearing in different places at the same time, or manifesting bodies of transformation. To gain these powers they even resort to the solitary life, but this class of masters never get beyond the seductions of their learning and egoism, and their discourses are always in conformity with that characteristic and limitation. Among them are many earnest disciples who show a degree of spiritual insight that is characterised by sincerity and undismayed willingness to meet all the demands that the stages make upon them. When they see that all that makes up the objective world is only manifestation of mind, that it is without self-nature, un-born and egoless, they accept it without fear, and when they see that their own ego-soul is also empty, un-born and egoless, they are untroubled and undismayed, with earnest purpose they seek to adjust their lives to the full demands of these truths, but they cannot forget the notions that lie back of these facts, especially the notion of their own conscious ego-self and its relation to Nirvana. They are of the Stream-entered class.

The class known as Arhats are those earnest masters who belong to the once-returning class. By their spiritual insight they have reached the sixth and seventh stages. They have thoroughly understood the truth of the twofold egolessness and the imagelessness. of Reality; with them there is no more discrimination, nor passions, nor pride of egoism; they have gained an exalted insight and seen into the immensity of the Buddha-lands. By attaining an inner perception of the true nature of Universal Mind they are steadily purifying their habit-energy. The Arhat has attained emancipation, enlightenment, the Dhyanas, the Samadhis, and his whole attention is given to the attainment of Nirvana, but the idea of Nirvana causes mental perturbations because he has a wrong idea of Nirvana. The notion of Nirvana in his mind is divided: he discriminates Nirvana from self, and self from others. He has attained some of the fruits of self-realisation but he still thinks and discourses on the Dhyanas, subjects for meditation, the Samadhis, the fruits. He pridefully says: "There are fetters, but I am disengaged from them." His is a double fault: he both denounces the vices of the ego, and still clings to its fetters. So long as he continues to discriminate notions of dhyana, dhyana practice, subjects for dhyana, right-knowledge and truth, there is a bewildered state of mind,—he has not attained perfect emancipation. Emancipation comes with the acceptance of imagelessness.

He is master of the Dhyanas and enters into the Samadhis, but to reach the higher stages one must pass beyond the Dhyanas, the immeasurables, the world of no-form, and the bliss of the Samadhis into the Samapattis leading to the cessation of thought itself. The dhyana-practiser, dhyana, the subject of dhyana, the cessation of thought, once-returning, never-returning, all these are divided and bewildering states of mind. Not until all discrimination is abandoned is their perfect emancipation. Thus the Arhat, master of the dhyanas, participating in the Samadhis, but unsupported by the Buddhas yields to the entrancing bliss of the Samadhis-and passes to his Nirvana. The Arhat is in the class of the Once-returning.

Disciples and masters and Arhats may ascend the stages up to the sixth. They perceive that the triple world is no more than mind itself; they perceive that there is no becoming attached to the multiplicities of external objects except through the discriminations and activities of the mind itself; they perceive that there is no ego-soul; and, therefore, they attain a measure of tranquillisation. But their tranquillisation is not perfect every minute of their lives, for with them there is something effect-producing, some grasped and grasping, some lingering trace of dualism and egoism. Though disengaged from the actively functioning passions, they are still bound in with the habit-energy of passion and, becoming intoxicated with the wine of the Samadhis, they still have their abode in the realm of the out-flowings. Perfect tranquillisation is possible only with the seventh stage. So long as their minds are in confusion, they cannot attain to a clear conviction as to the cessation of all multiplicity and the actuality of the perfect oneness of all things. In their minds the self-nature of things is still discriminated as good and bad, therefore, their minds are in confusion and they cannot pass beyond the sixth stage. But at the sixth stage all discrimination ceases as they become engrossed in the bliss of the Samadhis wherein they cherish the thought of Nirvana and, as Nirvana is possible at the sixth stage, they pass into their Nirvana, but it is not the Nirvana of the Buddhas.

Chapter XI

Bodhisattvahood and Its Stages

THEN SAID MAHAMATI to the Blessed One: Will you tell us now about the disciples who are Bodhisattvas?

The Blessed One replied: The Bodhisattvas are those earnest disciples who are enlightened by reason of their efforts to attain self-realisation of Noble Wisdom and who have taken upon themselves the task to enlighten others. They have gained a clear understanding of the truth that all things are empty, un-born, and of a maya-like nature; they have ceased from viewing things discriminatively and from considering them in their relations; they thoroughly understand the truth of twofold egolessness and have adjusted themselves to it with patient acceptance; they have attained a definite realisation of imagelessness; and they are abiding in the perfect-knowledge that they have gained by self-realisation of Noble Wisdom.

Well stamped by the seal of "Suchness" they entered upon the first of the Bodhisattva stages. The first stage is called the Stage of joy (*Pramudita*). Entering this stage is like passing out of the glare and shadows into a realm of "no-shadows"; it is like passing out of the noise and tumult of the crowded city into the quietness of solitude. The Bodhisattva feels within himself the awakening of a great heart of compassion and he utters his ten original vows: To honor and serve all Buddhas; to spread the knowledge and practice of the Dharma; to welcome all coming Buddhas; to practise the six Paramitas; to persuade all beings to embrace the Dharma; to attain a perfect understanding of the universe; to attain a perfect understanding of tile mutuality of all beings; to attain perfect self-realisation of the oneness of all the Buddhas and Tathagatas n self-nature, purpose and resources; to become acquainted with all skillful means for the carrying out of these vows for the emancipation of all beings; to realise supreme enlightenment through the perfect self-realisation of Noble Wisdom, ascending the stages and entering Tathagatahood.

In the spirit of these vows the Bodhisattva gradually ascends the stages to the sixth. All earnest disciples, masters and Arhats have ascended thus far, but being enchanted by the bliss of the Samadhis and not being supported by the powers of the Buddhas, they pass to their Nirvana. The same fate would befall the Bodhisattvas except for the sustaining power of the Buddhas, by that they are enabled to refuse to enter Nirvana until all beings can enter Nirvana with them. The Tathagatas point out to them the virtues of Buddhahood which are beyond the conception of the intellectual-mind, and they encourage and strengthen the Bodhisattvas not to give in to the enchantment of the bliss of the Samadhis, but to press on to further advancement along the stages. If the Bodhisattvas had entered Nirvana at this stage, and they would have done so without the sustaining power of the Buddhas, there would have been the cessation of all things and the family of the Tathagatas would have become extinct.

Strengthened by the new strength that comes to them from the Buddhas and with the more perfect insight that is theirs by reason of their advance in self-realisation of Noble Wisdom, they re-examine the nature of the mind-system, the egolessness of personality, and the part that grasping and attachment and habit-energy play in the unfolding drama of life; they re-examine the illusions of the fourfold logical analysis, and the various elements that enter into enlightenment and self-realisation, and, in the thrill of their new powers of self-mastery, the Bodhisattvas enter upon the seventh stage of Far-going (*Duramgama*).

Supported by the sustaining power of the Buddhas, the Bodhisattvas at this stage enter into the bliss of the Samadhi of perfect tranquillisation. Owing to their original vows they are transported by emotions of love and compassion as they become aware of the part they are to perform in the carrying out of their vows for the emancipation of all beings. Thus they do not enter into Nirvana, but, in truth, they too are already in Nirvana because in their emotions of love and compassion there is no rising of discrimination; henceforth, with them, discrimination no more takes place. Because of Transcendental Intelligence only one conception is present-the promotion of the realisation of Noble Wisdom. Their insight issues from the Womb of Tathagatahood and they enter into their task with spontaneity and radiancy because it is of the self-nature of Noble Wisdom. This is called the Bodhisattva's Nirvana-the losing oneself in the bliss of perfect self-yielding. This is the seventh stage, the stage of Far-going.

The eighth stage, is the stage of No-recession (*Acala*). Up to this stage, because of the defilements upon the face of Universal Mind caused by the accumulation of habit-energy since beginningless time, the mindsystem and all that pertains to it has been evolved and sustained. The mind-system functioned by the discriminations of an external and objective world to which it became attached and by which it was perpetuated. But with the Bodhisattva's attainment of the eighth stage there comes the "turning-about" within his deepest consciousness from self-centered egoism to universal compassion for all beings, by which he attains perfect self-realisation of Noble Wisdom. There is an instant cessation of the delusive activities of the whole mind-system; the dancing of the waves of habit-energy on the face of Universal Mind are forever stilled, revealing its own inherent quietness and solitude, the inconceivable Oneness of the Womb of Tathagatahood.

Henceforth there is no more looking outward upon an external world by senses and sense-minds, nor a discrimination of particularised concepts and ideas and propositions by an intellectual-mind, no more grasping, nor attachment, nor pride of egoism, nor habit-energy. Henceforth there is only the inner experience of Noble Wisdom which has been attained by entering into its perfect Oneness.

Thus establishing himself at the eighth stage of No-recession, the Bodhisattva enters into the bliss of the ten Samadhis, but avoiding the path of the disciples and masters who yielded themselves up to their entrancing bliss and who passed to their Nirvanas, and supported by his vows and the Transcendental Intelligence which now is his and being sustained by the power of the Buddhas, he enters upon the higher paths that lead to Tathagatahood. He passes through the bliss of the Samadhis to assume the transformation body of a Tathagata that through him all beings may be emancipated. Mahamati, If there had been no Tathagata-womb and no Divine Mind then there would have been no rising and disappearance of the aggregates that make up personality and its external world, no rising and disappearance of ignorant people nor holy people, and no task for Bodhisattvas; therefore, while walking in the path of self-realisation and entering into the enjoyments of the Samadhis, you must never abandon working hard for the emancipation of all beings and your self-yielding love will never be in vain. To philosophers the conception of Tathagata-womb seems devoid of purity and soiled by these external manifestations, but it is not so understood by the Tathagatas,—to them it is not a proposition of philosophy but is an intuitive experience as real as though it was an amalaka fruit held in the palm of the hand.

With the cessation of the mind-system and all its evolving discriminations, there is cessation of all strain and effort. It is like a man in a dream who imagines he is crossing a river and who exerts himself to the utmost to do so, who is suddenly awakened. Being awake, he thinks: "Is this real or is it unreal?" Being now enlightened, he knows that it is neither real nor unreal. Thus when the Bodhisattva arrives at the eighth stage, he is able to see all things truthfully and, more than that, he is able to thoroughly understand the significance of all the dream-like things of his life as to how they came to pass and as to how they pass away. Ever since beginningless time the mind-system has perceived multiplicities of forms and conditions and ideas which the thinking-mind has discriminated and the empirical-mind has experienced and grasped and clung to. From this has risen habit-energy that by its accumulation has conditioned the illusions of existence and non-existence, individuality and generality, and has thus perpetuated the dream-state of false-imagination. But now, to the Bodhisattvas of the eighth stage, life is past and is remembered as it truly was—a passing dream.

As long as the Bodhisattva had not passed the seventh stage, even though he had attained an intuitive understanding of the true meaning of life and its maya-like nature, and as to how the mind carried on its discriminations and attachments yet, nevertheless, the cherishing of the notions of these things had continued and, although he no longer experienced within himself any ardent desire for things nor any impulse to grasp them yet, nevertheless, the notions concerning them persisted and perfumed his efforts to practise the teachings of the Buddhas and to labor for the emancipation of all beings. Now, in the eighth stage, even the notions have passed away, and all effort and striving is seen to be unnecessary. The Bodhisattva's Nirvana is perfect tranquillisation, but it is not extinction nor inertness; while there is an entire absence of discrimination and purpose, there is the freedom and spontaneity of potentiality that has come with the attainment and patient acceptance of the truths of egolessness and imagelessness. Here is perfect solitude, undisturbed by any gradation or continuous succession, but radiant with the potency and freedom of its self-nature which is the self-nature of Noble Wisdom, blissfully peaceful with the serenity of Perfect Love.

Entering upon the eighth stage, with the turning-about at the deepest seat of consciousness, the Bodhisattva will become conscious that he has received the second kind of Transcendental-body (*Manomayakaya*). The transition from mortal-body to Transcendental-body has nothing to do with mortal death, for the old body continues to function and the old mind serves the needs of the old body, but now it is free from the control of mortal mind. There has been an inconceivable transformation-death (*acintya-parinama-cyuti*) by which the false-imagination of his particularised individual personality has been transcended by a realisation of his oneness with the universalised mind of Tathagatahood, from which realisation there will be no recession. With that realisation he finds himself amply endowed with all the Tathagata's powers, psychic faculties, and self-mastery, and, just as the good earth is the support of all beings in the world of desire (*karmadhatu*), so the Tathagatas become the support of all beings in the Transcendental World of No-form.

The first seven of the Bodhisattva stages were in the realm of mind and the eighth, while transcending mind, was still in touch with it; but in the ninth stage of Transcendental Intelligence (*Sadhumati*), by reason of his perfect intelligence and insight into the imagelessness of Divine Mind which he had attained by self-realisation of Noble Wisdom, he is in the realm of Tathagatahood. Gradually the Bodhisattva will realise his Tathagata-nature and the possession of all its powers and psychic faculties, self-mastery, loving compassion, and skillful means, and by means of them will enter into all the Buddha-lands. Making use of these new powers, the Bodhisattva will assume various transformation-bodies and personalities for the sake of benefiting others. Just as in the former mental life, imagination had risen from relative-knowledge, so now skillful-means rise spontaneously from Transcendental Intelligence. It is like the magical gem that reflects instantaneously appropriate responses to one's wishes. The Bodhisattva passes over to all the assemblages of the Buddhas and listens to them as they discourse on the dream-like nature of all things and concerning the truths that transcend all notions of being and nonbeing, that have no relation to birth and death, nor to eternality nor extinction. Thus facing the Tathagatas as they discourse on Noble Wisdom that is far beyond the mental capacity of disciples and masters, he will attain a hundred thousand Samadhis, indeed, a hundred thousand nyutas of kotis of Samadhis, and in the spirit of these Samadhis he will instantly pass from one Buddha-land to another, paying homage to all the Buddhas, being born into all the celestial mansions, manifesting Buddha-bodies, and himself discoursing on the Triple Treasure to lesser Bodhisattvas that they too may partake of the fruits of self-realisation of Noble Wisdom.

Thus passing beyond the last stage of Bodhisattvahood, he becomes a Tathagata himself endowed with all the freedom of the Dharmakaya. The tenth stage belongs to the Tathagatas. Here the Bodhisattva will find himself seated upon a lotus-like throne in a splendid jewel-adorned palace and surrounded by Bodhisattvas of equal rank. Buddhas from all the Buddha-lands will gather about him and with their pure and fragrant hands resting on his forehead will give him ordination and recognition as one of themselves. Then they will assign him a Buddha-land that he may possess and perfect as his own.

The tenth stage is called the Great Truth Cloud (*Dharmamegha*), inconceivable, inscrutable. Only the Tathagatas can realise its perfect Imagelessness and Oneness and Solitude. It is Mahesvara, the Radiant Land, the Pure Land, the Land of Far-distances; surrounding and surpassing the lesser worlds of form and desire (*karmadhatu*), in which the Bodhisattva will find himself at-one-ment. Its rays of Noble Wisdom which is the self-nature of the Tathagatas, many-colored, entrancing, auspicious, are transforming the triple world as other worlds have been transformed in the past, and still other worlds will be transformed in the future. But in the Perfect Oneness of Noble Wisdom there is no gradation nor succession nor effort, The tenth stage is the first, the first is the eighth, the eighth is the fifth, the fifth is the seventh: what gradation can there be where perfect Imagelessness and Oneness prevail? And what is the reality of Noble Wisdom? It is the ineffable potency of the Dharmakaya; it has no bounds nor limits; It surpasses all the Buddha-lands, and pervades the Akanistha and the heavenly mansions of the Tushita.

Chapter XII

Tathagatahood Which Is Noble Wisdom

THEN SAID MAHAMATI to the Blessed One: it has been taught in the canonical books that the Buddhas are subject to neither birth nor destruction, and you have said that "the Unborn" is one of the names of the Tathagatas; does that mean that the Tathagata is a non-entity?

The Blessed One replied: The Tathagata is not a non-entity nor is he to be conceived as other things are as neither born nor disappearing, nor is he subject to causation, nor is he without significance; yet I refer to him as "The Un-born." There is yet another name for the Tathagata, "The Mind-appearing One" (*Manomayakaya*) which his Essence-body assumes at will in the transformations incident to his work of emancipation. This is beyond the understanding of common disciples and masters and even beyond the full comprehension of those Bodhisattvas who remain in the seventh stage. Yes, Mahamati, "The Un-born" is synonymous with Tathagata.

Then Mahamati said: If the Tathagatas are un-born, there does not seem to be anything to take hold of—no entity—or is there something that bears another name than entity? And what can that "something" be?

The Blessed One replied: Objects are frequently known by different names according to different aspects that they present,—the god Indra is sometimes known as Shakra, and sometimes as Purandara. These different names are sometimes used interchangeably and sometimes they are discriminated, but different objects are not to be imagined because of the different names, nor are they without individuation. The same can be said of myself as I appear in this world of patience before ignorant people and where I am known by uncounted trillions of names. They address me by different names not realising that they are all names of the one Tathagata. Some recognise me as Tathagata, some as The Self-existent One, some as Gautama the Ascetic, some as Buddha. Then there are others who recognise me as Brahma, as Vishnu, as Ishvara; some see me as Sun, as Moon; some as a reincarnation of the ancient sages; some as one of "the ten powers"; some as Rama, some as Indra, and some as Varuna. Still there are others who speak of me as The Un-born, as Emptiness, as "Suchness," as Truth, as Reality, as Ultimate Principle; still there are others who see me as Dharmakaya, as Nirvana, as the Eternal; some speak of me as sameness, as non-duality, as undying, as formless; some think of me as the doctrine of Buddha-causation, or of Emancipation, or of the Noble Path; and some think of me as Divine Mind and Noble Wisdom. Thus in this world and in other worlds am I known by these uncounted names, but they all see me as the moon is seen in water. Though they all honor, praise and esteem me, they do not fully understand the meaning and significance of the words they use;

not having their own self-realisation of Truth they cling to the words of their canonical books, or to what has been told them, or to what they have imagined, and fail to see that the name they are using is only one of the many names of the Tathagata. In their studies they follow the mere words of the text vainly trying to gain the true meaning, instead of having confidence in the one "text" where self-confirming Truth is revealed, that is, having confidence in the self-realisation of Noble Wisdom.

THEN SAID MAHAMATI: Pray tell us, Blessed One about the self-nature of the Tathagatas?

The Blessed One replied: If the Tathagata is to be described by such expressions as made or un-made, effect or cause, we would have to describe him as neither made, nor un-made, nor effect, nor cause; but if we so described him we would be guilty of dualistic discrimination. If the Tathagata is something made, he would be impermanent; if he is impermanent anything made would be a Tathagata. If he is something un-made, then all effort to realise Tathagatahood would be useless. That which is neither an effect nor a cause, is neither a being nor a non-being, and that which is neither a being nor a non-being is outside the four propositions. The four propositions belong to worldly usage; that which is outside them is no more than a word, like a barren-woman's child; so are all the terms concerning the Tathagata to be understood.

When it is said that all things are egoless, it means that all things are devoid of self-hood. Each thing may have its own individuality—the being of a horse is not of cow nature—it is such as it is of its own nature and is thus discriminated by the ignorant, but, nevertheless, its own nature is of the nature of a dream or a vision.

That is why the ignorant and the simple-minded, who are in the habit of discriminating appearances, fail to understand the significance of egolessness. It is not until discrimination is gotten rid of that the fact that all things are empty, un-born and without self-nature can be appreciated.

Mahamati, all these expressions as applied to the Tathagatas are without meaning, for that which is none of these is something removed from all measurement, and that which is removed from all measurement turns into a meaningless word; that which is a mere word is something un-born; that which is unborn is not subject to destruction; that which is not subject to destruction is like space and space is neither effect nor cause; that which is neither effect nor cause is something unconditioned; that which is unconditioned is beyond all reasoning; that which is beyond all reasoning,—that is the Tathagata. The self-nature of Tathagatahood is far removed from all predicates and measurements; the self-nature of Tathagatahood is Noble Wisdom.

THEN MAHAMATI SAID to the Blessed One: Are the Tathagatas permanent or impermanent?

The Blessed One replied: The Tathagatas are neither permanent nor impermanent; if either is asserted there is error connected with it. If the

Tathagata is said to be permanent then he will be connected with the creating agencies for, according to the philosophers, the creating agencies are something uncreated and permanent. But the Tathagatas are not connected with the so-called creating agencies and in that sense he is impermanent. If he is said to be impermanent then he is connected with things that are created for they also are impermanent. For these reasons the Tathagatas are neither permanent nor impermanent.

Neither can the Tathagatas he said to be permanent in the sense that space is said to be permanent, or that the horns of a hare can be said to be permanent for, being unreal, they exclude all ideas of permanency or impermanency. This does not apply to the Tathagatas because they come forth from the habit-energy of ignorance which is connected with the mind-system and the elements that make up personality. The triple world originates from the discrimination of unrealities and where discrimination takes place there is duality and the notion of permanency and impermanency, but the Tathagatas do not rise from the discrimination of unrealities. Thus, as long as there is discrimination there will be the notion of permanency and impermanency; when discrimination is done away with, Noble Wisdom, which is based on the significance of solitude, will be established.

However, there is another sense in which the Tathagatas may be said to be permanent. Transcendental Intelligence rising with the attainment of enlightenment is of a permanent nature. This Truth-essence which is discoverable in the enlightenment of all who are enlightened, is realisable as the regulative and sustaining principle of Reality, which forever abides. The Transcendental Intelligence attained intuitively by the Tathagatas by their self-realisation of Noble Wisdom, is a realisation of their own self-nature,—in this sense the Tathagatas are permanent. The eternal-unthinkable of the Tathagatas is the "suchness" of Noble Wisdom realised within themselves. It is both eternal and beyond thought. It conforms to the idea of a cause and yet is beyond existence and non-existence. Because it is the exalted state of Noble-Wisdom, it has its own character. Because it is the cause of highest Reality, it is its own causation. Its eternality is not derived from reasonings based on external notions of being and non-being, nor of eternality nor non-eternality. Being classed under the same head as space, cessasion, Nirvana, it is eternal. Because it has nothing to do with existence and non-existence, it is no creator; because it has nothing to do with creation, nor with being and non-being, but is only revealed in the exalted state of Noble Wisdom, it is truly eternal.

When the twofold passions are destroyed, and the twofold hindrances are cleared away, and the twofold egolessness is fully understood, and the inconceivable transformation death of the Bodhisattva is attained—that which remains is the self-nature of the Tathagatas. When the teachings of the Dharma are fully understood and are perfectly realised by the disciples and masters, that which is realised in their deepest consciousness is their own Buddha-nature revealed as Tathagata.

In a true sense there are four kinds of sameness relating to Buddha-nature: there is sameness of letters, sameness of words, sameness of meaning, and sameness of Essence. The name Buddha is spelt: B-U-D-D-H-A; the letters are the same when used for any Buddha or Tathagata. When the Brahmans teach they use various words, and when the Tathagatas teach they use the very same words; in respect to words there is a sameness between us. In the teachings of all the Tathagatas there is a sameness of meaning. Among all the Buddhas there is a sameness of Buddha-nature. They all have the thirty-two marks of excellence and the eighty minor signs of bodily perfection; there is no distinction among them except as they manifest various transformations according to the different dispositions of beings who are to be disciplined and emancipated by various means. In the Ultimate Essence which is Dharmakaya, all the Buddhas of the past, present and future, are of one sameness.

THEN SAID MAHAMATI to the Blessed One: It has been said by the Blessed One that from the night of the Enlightenment to the night of the Parinirvana, the Tathagata has uttered no word nor ever will utter a word. In what deep meaning is this true?

The Blessed One replied: By two reasons of deepest meaning is it true: In the light of the Truth self-realised by Noble Wisdom; and in the Truth of an eternally-abiding Reality. The self-realisation of Noble Wisdom by all the Tathagatas is the same as my own self-realisation of Noble Wisdom; there is no more, no less, no difference; and all the Tathagatas bear witness that the state of self-realisation is free from words and discriminations and has nothing to do with the dualistic way of speaking, that is, all beings receive the teachings of the Tathagatas through self-realisation of Noble Wisdom, not through words of discrimination.

Again, Mahamati, there has always been an eternally-abiding Reality. The "substance" of Truth (*dharmadhatu*) abides forever whether a Tathagata appears in the world or not. So does the Reason of all things (*dharmata*) eternally abide; so does Reality (paramartha) abide and keep its order. What has been realised by myself and all other Tathagatas is this Reality (*Dharmakaya*), the eternally-abiding self-orderliness of Reality; the "suchness" (*tathata*) of things; the realness of things (*bhutata*); Noble Wisdom which is Truth itself. The sun radiates its splendor spontaneously on all alike and with no words of explanation; in like manner do the Tathagatas radiate the Truth of Noble Wisdom with no recourse to words and to all alike. For these reasons is it stated by me that from the night of the Enlightenment to the night of the Tathagata's Parinirvana, he has not uttered, nor ever will he utter, one word. And the same is true of all the Buddhas.

THEN SAID MAHAMATI: Blessed One, you speak of the sameness of all the Buddhas, but in other places you have spoken of Dharmata-Buddha, Nishyanda-Buddha and Nirmana-Buddha as though they were different from each other; how can they be the same and yet different?

The Blessed One replied: I speak of the different Buddhas as opposed to the views of the philosophers who base their teachings on the reality of an external world of form and who cherish discriminations and attachments arising therefrom; against the teachings of these philosophers I disclose the Nirmana-Buddha, the Buddha of Transformations. In the many transformations of the Tathagata stage, the Nirmana-Buddha establishes such matters as charity, morality, patience, thoughtfulness, and tranquillisation; by right-knowledge he teaches the true understanding of the maya-like nature of the elements that make up personality and its external world; he teaches the true nature of the mind-system as a whole and in the distinctions of its forms, functions and ways of performance. In a deeper sense, The Nirmana-Buddha symbolises the principles of differentiation and integration by reason of which all component things are distributed, all complexities simplified, all thoughts analysed; at the same time it symbolises the harmonising, unifying power of sympathy and compassion; it removes all obstacles, it harmonises all differences, it brings into perfect Oneness the discordant many. For the emancipation of all beings the Bodhisattvas and Tathagatas assume bodies of transformation and employ many skillful devices,—this is the work of the Nirmana-Buddha.

For the enlightenment of the Bodhisattvas and their sustaining along the stages, the Inconceivable is made realisable. The Nishyanda-Buddha, the "Out-flowing-Buddha," through Transcendental Intelligence, reveals the true meaning and significance of appearances, discrimination, attachment; and of the power of habit-energy which is accumulated by them and conditions them; and of the un-bornness the emptiness, the egolessness of all things. Because of Transcendental Intelligence and the purification of the evil out-flowings of life, all dualistic views of existence and nonexistence are transcended and by self-realisation of Noble Wisdom the true imagelessness of Reality is made manifest. The inconceivable glory of Buddhahood is made manifest in rays of Noble Wisdom; Noble Wisdom is the self-nature of the Tathagatas. This is the work of the Nishyanda-Buddha. In a deeper sense, the Nishyanda-Buddha symbolises the emergence of the principles of intellection and compassion but as yet undifferentiated and in perfect balance, potential but unmanifest. Looked at from the in-going side of the Bodhisattvas, Nishyanda-Buddha is seen in the glorified bodies of the Tathagatas; looked at from the forth-going side of Buddhahood, Nishyanda-Buddha is seen in the radiant personalities of the Tathagatas ready and eager to manifest the inherent Love and Wisdom of the Dharmakaya.

Dharmata-Buddha is Buddhahood in its self-nature of Perfect Oneness in whom absolute tranquillity prevails. As Noble Wisdom, Dharmata-Buddha transcends all differentiated knowledge, is the goal of intuitive self-realisation, and is the self-nature of the Tathagatas. As Noble Wisdom, Dharmata-Buddha is inscrutable, ineffable, unconditioned. Dharmata-Buddha is the Ultimate Principle of Reality from which all things derive their being and truthfulness, but which in itself transcends all predicates. Dharmata-Buddha is the central sun which holds all, illumines all. Its inconceivable Essence is made manifest in the "out-flowing" glory of Nishyanda-Buddha and in the transformations of Nirmana-Buddha.

THEN SAID MAHAMATI: Pray tell us, Blessed One, more about the Dharmakaya?

The Blessed One replied: We have been speaking of it in terms of Buddhahood, but as it is inscrutable and beyond predicate we may just as well speak of it as the Truth-body, or the Truth-principle of Ultimate Reality (*Paramartha*). This Ultimate Principle of Reality may be considered as it is manifested under seven aspects: First, as Citta-gocara, it is the world of spiritual experience and the abode of the Tathagatas on their outgoing mission of emancipation. It is Noble Wisdom manifested as the principle of irradiancy and individuation. Second, as Jnana, it is the mind-world and its principle of intellection and consciousness. Third, as Dristi, it is the realm of dualism which is the physical world of birth and death wherein are manifested all the differentiations of thinker, thinking and thought-about and wherein are manifested the principles of sensation, perception, discrimination, desire, attachment and suffering.

Fourth, because of the greed, anger, infatuation, suffering and need of the physical world incident to discrimination and attachment, it reveals a world beyond the realm of dualism wherein it appears as the integrating principle of charity and sympathy. Fifth, in a realm still higher, which is the abode of the Bodhisattva stages, and is analogous to the mind-world, where the interests of heart transcend those of the mind, it appears as the principle of compassion and self-giving. Sixth, in the spiritual realm where the Bodhisattvas attain Buddhahood, it appears as the principle of perfect Love (*Karuna*). Here the last clinging to an ego-self is abandoned and the Bodhisattva enters into his self-realisation of Noble Wisdom which is the bliss of the Tathagata's perfect enjoyment of his inmost nature. Seventh, as Prajna it is the active aspect of the Ultimate Principle wherein both the forth-going and the in-coming principles are alike, implicit and potential, and wherein both Wisdom and Love are in perfect balance, harmony and Oneness.

These are the seven aspects of the Ultimate Principle of Dharmakaya, by reason of which all things are made manifest and perfected and then reintegrated, and all remaining within its inscrutable Oneness, with no signs of individuation, nor beginning, nor succession, nor ending. We speak of it as Dharmakaya, as Ultimate Principle, as Buddhahood, as Nirvana; what matters it? They are only other names for Noble Wisdom.

Mahamati, you and all the Bodhisattva-Mahasattvas should avoid the erroneous reasonings of the philosophers and seek for a self-realisation of Noble Wisdom.

Chapter XIII
Nirvana

THEN SAID MAHAMATI to the Blessed One: Pray tell Us about Nirvana?

The Blessed One replied: The term, Nirvana, is used with many different meanings, by different people, but these people may be divided into four groups: There are people who are suffering, or who are afraid of suffering, and who think of Nirvana; there are the philosophers who try to discriminate Nirvana; there are the class of disciples who think of Nirvana in relation to themselves; and, finally there is the Nirvana of the Buddhas.

Those who are suffering or who fear suffering, think of Nirvana as an escape and a recompense. They imagine that Nirvana consists in the future annihilation of the senses and the sense-minds; they are not aware that Universal Mind and Nirvana are One, and that this life-and-death world and Nirvana are not to be separated. These ignorant ones, instead of meditating on the imagelessness of Nirvana, talk of different ways of emancipation. Being ignorant of, or not understanding, the teachings of the Tathagatas, they cling to the notion of Nirvana that is outside what is seen of the mind and, thus, go on rolling themselves along with the wheel of life and death.

As to the Nirvanas discriminated by the philosophers: there really are none. Some philosophers conceive Nirvana to be found where the mind-system no more operates owing to the cessation of the elements that make up personality and its world; or is found where there is utter indifference to the objective world and its impermanency. Some conceive Nirvana to be a state where there is no recollection of the past or present, just as when a lamp is extinguished, or when a seed is burnt, or when a fire goes out; because then there is the cessation of all the substrate, which is explained by the philosophers as the non-rising of discrimination. But this is not Nirvana, because Nirvana does not consist in simple annihilation and vacuity.

Again, some philosophers explain deliverance as though it was the mere stopping of discrimination, as when the wind stops blowing, or as when one by self-effort gets rid of the dualistic view of knower and known, or gets rid of the notions of permanency and impermanency; or gets rid of the notions of good and evil; or overcomes passion by means of knowledge;—to them Nirvana is deliverance. Some, seeing in "form" the bearer of pain are alarmed by the notion of "form" and look for happiness in a world of "no-form." Some conceive that in consideration of individuality and generality recognisable in all things inner and outer, that there is no destruction and that all beings maintain their being for ever and, in this eternality, see Nirvana. Others see the eternality of things in the conception of Nirvana as the absorption of the finite-soul in Supreme Atman; or who see all things as a manifestation of the vital-force of some Supreme Spirit to which all return; and some, who are especially silly, declare that there are two primary things, a primary substance and a primary soul, that react differently upon each other and thus produce all things from the transformations of qualities; some think that the world is born of action and interaction and that no other cause is necessary; others think that Ishvara is the free creator of all things; clinging to these foolish notions, there is no awakening, and they consider Nirvana to consist in the fact that there is no awakening.

Some imagine that Nirvana is where self-nature exists in its own right, unhampered by other self-natures, as the varigated feathers of a peacock, or various precious crystals, or the pointedness of a thorn. Some conceive being to be Nirvana, some non-being, while others conceive that all things and Nirvana are not to be distinguished from one another. Some, thinking that time is the creator and that as the rise of the world depends on time, they conceive that Nirvana consists in the recognition of time as Nirvana. Some think that there will be Nirvana when the "twenty-five" truths are generally accepted, or when the king observes the six virtues, and some religionists think that Nirvana is the attainment of paradise.

These views severally advanced by the philosophers with their various reasonings are not in accord with logic nor are they acceptable to the wise. They all conceive Nirvana dualistically and in some causal connection; by these discriminations philosophers imagine Nirvana, but where there is no rising and no disappearing, how can there be discrimination? Each philosopher relying on his own textbook from which he draws his understanding, sins against the truth, because truth is not where he imagines it to be. The only result is that it sets his mind to wandering about and becoming more confused as Nirvana is not to be found by mental searching, and the more his mind becomes confused the more he confuses other people.

As to the notion of Nirvana as held by disciples and masters who still cling to the notion of an ego-self, and who try to find it by going off by themselves into solitude: their notion of Nirvana is an eternity of bliss like the bliss of the Samadhis-for themselves. They recognise that the world is only a manifestation of mind and that all discriminations are of the mind, and so they forsake social relations and practise various spiritual disciplines and in solitude seek self-realisation of Noble Wisdom by self-effort. They follow the stages to the sixth and attain the bliss of the Samadhis, but as they are still clinging to egoism they do not attain the "turning-about" at the deepest seat of consciousness and, therefore, they are not free from the thinking-mind and the accumulation of its habit-energy. Clinging to the bliss of the Samadhis, they pass to their Nirvana, but it is not the Nirvana of the Tathagatas. They are of those who have "entered the stream"; they must return to this world of life and death.

THEN SAID MAHAMATI to the Blessed One: When the Bodhisattvas yield up their stock of merit for the emancipation of all beings, they become spiritually one with all animate life; they themselves may be purified, but in others there yet remain unexhausted evil and unmatured karma. Pray tell us, Blessed One, how the Bodhisattvas are given assurance of Nirvana? and what is the Nirvana of the Bodhisattvas?

The Blessed One replied: Mahamati, this assurance is not an assurance of numbers nor logic; it is not the mind that is to be assured but the heart. The Bodhisattva's assurance comes with the unfolding insight that follows passion hindrances cleared away, knowledge hindrance purified, and egolessness clearly perceived and patiently accepted. As the mortal-mind ceases to discriminate, there is no more thirst for life, no more sex-lust, no more thirst for learning, no more thirst for eternal life; with the disappearance of these fourfold thirsts, there is no more accumulation of habit-energy; with no more accumulation of habit-energy the defilements on the face of Universal Mind clear away, and the Bodhisattva attains self-realisation of Noble Wisdom that is the heart's assurance of Nirvana.

There are Bodhisattvas here and in other Buddha-lands, who are sincerely devoted to the Bodhisattva's mission and yet who cannot wholly forget the bliss of the Samadhis and the peace of Nirvana-for themselves. The teaching of Nirvana in which there is no substrate left behind, is revealed according to a hidden meaning for the sake of these disciples who still cling to thoughts of Nirvana for themselves, that they may be inspired to exert themselves in the Bodhisattva's mission of emancipation for all beings. The Transformation-Buddhas teach a doctrine of Nirvana to meet conditions as they find them, and to give encouragement to the timid and selfish. In order to turn their thoughts away from themselves and to encourage them to a deeper compassion and more earnest zeal for others, they are given assurance as to the future by the sustaining power of the Buddhas of Transformation, but not by the Dharmata-Buddha.

The Dharma which establishes the Truth of Noble Wisdom belongs to the realm of the Dharmata-Buddha. To the Bodhisattvas of the seventh and eighth stages, Transcendental Intelligence is revealed by the Dharmata-Buddha and the Path is pointed out to them which they are to follow. In the perfect self-realisation of Noble Wisdom that follows the inconceivable transformation death of the Bodhisattva's individualised will-control, he no longer lives unto himself, but the life that he lives thereafter is the Tathagata's universalised life as manifested in its transformations. In this perfect self-realisation of Noble Wisdom the Bodhisattva realises that for Buddhas there is no Nirvana.

The death of a Buddha, the great Parinirvana, is neither destruction nor death, else would it be birth and continuation. If it were destruction, it would be an effect-producing deed, which it is not. Neither is it a vanishing nor an abandonment, neither is it attainment, nor is it of no attainment;

neither is it of one significance nor of no significance, for there is no Nirvana for the Buddhas.

The Tathagata's Nirvana is where it is recognised that there is nothing but what is seen of the mind itself; is where, recognising the nature of the self-mind, one no longer cherishes the dualisms of discrimination; is where there is no more thirst nor grasping; is where there is no more attachment to external things. Nirvana is where the thinking-mind with all its discriminations, attachments, aversions and egoism is forever put away; is where logical measures, as they are seen to be inert, are no longer seized upon; is where even the notion of truth is treated with indifference because of its causing bewilderment; is where, getting rid of the four propositions, there is insight into the abode of Reality. Nirvana is where the twofold passions have subsided and the twofold hindrances are cleared away and the twofold egolessness is patiently accepted; is where, by the attainment of the "turning-about" in the deepest seat of consciousness, self-realisation of Noble Wisdom is fully entered into,—that is the Nirvana of the Tathagatas. Nirvana is where the Bodhisattva stages are passed one after another; is where the sustaining power of the Buddhas upholds the Bodhisattvas in the bliss of the Samadhis; is where compassion for others transcends all thoughts of self; is where the Tathagata stage is finally realised.

Nirvana is the realm of Dharmata-Buddha; it is where the manifestation of Noble Wisdom that is Buddhahood expresses itself in Perfect Love for all; it is where the manifestation of Perfect Love that is Tathagatahood expresses itself in Noble Wisdom for the enlightenment of all;—there, indeed, is Nirvana!

There are two classes of those who may not enter the Nirvana of the Tathagatas: there are those who have abandoned the Bodhisattva ideals, saying, they are not in conformity with the sutras, the codes of morality, nor with emancipation. Then there are the true Bodhisattvas who, on account of their original vows made for the sake of all beings, saying, "So long as they do not attain Nirvana, I will not attain it myself," voluntarily keep themselves out of Nirvana. But no beings are left outside by the will of the Tathagatas; some day each and every one will be influenced by the wisdom and love of the Tathagatas of Transformation to lay up a stock of merit and ascend the stages. But, if they only realised it, they are already in the Tathagata's Nirvana for, in Noble Wisdom, all things are in Nirvana from the beginning.

The
Diamond Sutra

Based on William Gemmell's Translation Edited,
Rearranged and Interpreted

Preface

THIS VERSION is based upon the English translation by William Gemmell, of the Chinese translation made by Kumarajiva, and was published by Kegan Paul in 1912. It is not an exact translation of the Chinese but is in a measure interpreted; it is very well done and proved to be more suitable for the present purpose than Max Muller's more scholarly one which was made direct from the Sanskrit original text.

There is no knowledge as to its author nor as to the date of its composition, but it must have been written about the beginning of the Christian era. It is the ninth section of a much larger treatise entitled: Mahaprajnaparamita Sutra. It is very metaphysical and difficult reading, but has always been very highly valued by Buddhist scholars. Apparently the text had become more or less confused long before the Chinese translations were made, so that in its present form there is little progressive unfolding of the theme. The Truth is there but it takes a scholar to dig it out. In this Version, the editor interprets its theme to be: The observance of the Six Paramitas in the light of the fundamental Dharma of emptiness and egolessness. With this in mind the Sutra has been rearranged and divided into sections and freely interpreted. To bring its teaching into clear and emphatic notice, quotations have been made from THE AWAKENING OF FAITH SUTRA to provide definitions of the Paramitas and they have been inserted near the head of each section.

As explained in the Preface to the Self-realisation of Noble Wisdom, this Sutra was greatly used from the very beginning by the founders of the Zen Sect concurrently with the LANKAVATARA, but because of the greater difficulties of the latter, it gradually displaced it, and after the Tenth Century was almost exclusively used as its chief Sutra. Its chief teaching that all phenomenal things and definitive ideas are subjective and a manifestation of one's own mind, that even the Scriptures are "empty," largely explains the characteristic tenets of the Zen Sect:

"A special transmission outside the Scriptures; No dependence upon words and letters; Direct pointing to one's deepest consciousness; Seeing into one's nature and the attainment of Buddhahood."

The Sutra teaches, according to Max Muller, "In contradistinction to the fallacious phenomena, there is the true essence of mind. Underlying the phenomena of mind, there is an unchanging principle." This is true, but the Sutra also teaches that all good disciples should practice the Paramitas in the light of it.

The Diamond Scripture
(Vajracchedika Sutra)

THUS HAVE I HEARD. Upon a memorable occasion, the Lord Buddha sojourned in the kingdom of Shravasti, lodging in the grove of Jeta, a park within the royal domain which Jeta, the heir-apparent, had bestowed upon Sutana, a minister of state renouned for his charities and benefactions. With the Lord Buddha there were assembled twelve hundred and fifty mendicant disciples, besides many who had attained to eminent degrees of spiritual wisdom.

As the hour for the morning meal approached, Lord Buddha attired in a mendicant's robe and carrying an alms bowl, walked towards the great cry of Shravasti which he entered to beg for food. Within the city he went from door to door and received such gifts as the good people severally bestowed. Concluding this religious exercise, the Lord Buddha returned to the grove of Jeta and after bathing his sacred feet partook of the frugal meal which he had received as alms. Thereafter he divested himself of the mendicant's robe, laid aside the alms bowl and accepted the seat of honor which his disciples had reserved for him.

The venerable Subhuti, who occupied a place in the midst of the assembly, rose from his seat, arranged his robe so that his right shoulder was exposed, pressing the palms of his hands together, and kneeling upon his right knee, respectfully bowed to the Lord Buddha, saying: "Thou art of transcendent wisdom, Honored of the Worlds! With wonderful solicitude thou dost instruct in the Dharma and preserve in the faith this illustrious assembly of enlightened disciples. Blessed One, may I beseech of you to discourse upon the theme: How should a disciple who has entered upon the path behave? How should he advance? How should he restrain his thoughts? How may he realise Buddhahood? What immutable Truth is there that shall sustain the mind of a good disciple, who is seeking to attain supreme spiritual wisdom, and bring into subjection every inordinate desire?"

The Lord Buddha replied to Sabuti, saying: "Truly a most excellent theme. Attend diligently unto me and I will enunciate a Truth whereby the mind of a good disciple, whether man or woman, seeking to attain supreme spiritual wisdom shall be adequately sustained and enabled to bring into subjection every inordinate desire.

"Subhuti, it is by the Truth of emptiness and egolessness that enlightened disciples are to advance along the Path, to restrain their thoughts, to attain Buddhahood. If they diligently observe the Paramitas, and fully enter into a realisation of the profound Prajna Paramita, they will attain the supreme spiritual wisdom they seek."

DANA PARAMITA—IDEAL CHARITY

"Subhuti, good disciples, whether man or woman, should thus arrange their thoughts. Every species of life whether hatched in an egg, formed in a womb, evolved from spawn, produced by metamorphosis, with or without form, possessing or devoid of natural instinct or intelligence,—from these changeful conditions of being, I urge you to seek deliverance in the transcendental concept of Nirvana. Thus shall disciples be delivered from the immeasurable, innumerable, and illimitable world of sentient life, but, in reality, there is no world of sentient life from which to seek deliverance. And why? Because, in the minds of enlightened disciples there have ceased to exist such arbitrary concepts of phenomena as an entity, a being, a living being, a personality."

(Subhuti, regarding the Dana Paramita—Ideal Charity, the Awakening of Faith Scripture teaches how disciples should practise charity. It says: "If persons should come to them and ask for something, they should as far as their means allow, supply it ungrudgingly and thus make them happy. If they see people threatened with danger, they should try every means for rescuing them and restore them to a feeling of safety. If people come to them desiring instruction in the Dharma, they should, as far as they are acquainted with it and according to their discretion, deliver discourses upon religious themes. And when they are performing these acts of charity, let them not cherish any desire for fame or advantage, nor covet any earthly reward. Thinking only of the benefits and blessings that are to be mutually shared, let them aspire for the most excellent, the most perfect wisdom.")

The Lord Buddha resumed: "Moreover, Subhuti, an enlightened disciple in his acts of charity, ought to act spontaneously, uninfluenced by such things as form, sound, taste, odour, touch, discrimination, and favoritism. It is imperative that an enlightened disciple, in the exercise of charity, should act independent of phenomena. And why? Because, acting without regard to illusive forms of phenomena, he will realise in the exercise of charity a merit inestimable and immeasurable.

"Subhuti, what think you? Is it possible to estimate the distances that comprise the illimitable universe of space?"

Subhuti replied: "Blessed One! It is impossible to estimate the distances comprising the illimitable universe of space."

The Lord Buddha continued: "It is equally impossible to estimate the merit of an enlightened disciple who practises charity unperturbed by the disturbing influences of Phenomena. Subhuti, the minds of all disciples ought thus to be taught."

SILA PARAMITA—IDEAL BEHAVIOR

The Lord Buddha addressing Subhuti, said: "What think you? If a benevolent person bestowed as alms an abundance of the seven treasures sufficient to fill the universe, would there accrue to that person a considerable merit?"

Subhuti replied, saying: "A very considerable merit; Honored of the Worlds! Because what is referred to does not partake of the nature of ordinary merit; in that sense the Lord Buddha rightly speaks of 'a considerable merit.'"

The Lord Buddha continued: "If a disciple studies and adheres with implicit faith to even a stanza of this Scripture, the intrinsic merit of such a disciple would be relatively greater. And why? Because, the Tathagatas who have attained supreme spiritual wisdom, all owe their beginning to the Truth of this sacred Scripture—the Truth of Emptiness and Egolessness."

(Regarding the Sila Paramita—Ideal Behavior—the Sutra says: "Lay members should abstain from all unkindness, stealing, unchastity, lying, duplicity, slander, frivolous talk, covetousness, malice, currying favor, and false teachings. Disciples, in order to disarm prejudice, should retire from the excitement of the worldly life and, abiding in solitude, should practise those deeds which lead to restraint and contentment. In the case of advanced bhikshus, they have other rules to follow and should feel all the more shame, fear and remorse for any failure to observe the minor precepts. Strictly observing all the precepts given by the Tathagatas, they should endeavor, by their example, to induce all beings to abandon evil and practise the good.")

"What do you think, Subhuti? If a disciple, whether man or woman, were to collect a store of precious gems as great as this universe and was to bestow them on the holy Tathagatas, would that disciple on the strength of his gift lay up a large stock of merit?"

Subhuti replied: "Yes, Blessed One, he would lay up a very great merit."

The Lord Buddha replied: "Subhuti, if another disciple after reading even one verse of this Scripture and observing it by living a good life, he will lay up a greater merit than the one who merely makes gifts in charity and continues his egoistic life. And why? Because, making gifts may or may not involve an advance along the Path that leads to Nirvana, but this Scripture points the way to the stages of Bodhisattvahood and the supreme spiritual enlightenment of the Buddhas. The disciple who sincerely reads this Scripture and lives a virtuous life is laying up merit immeasurable. But, Subhuti, a virtuous life, even the life of a Buddha, what is it? There is no such thing, it is only a name.

"Subhuti, suppose a man had a body as large as Mount Sumeru, would he be counted a great man?"

Subhuti replied: "Exceedingly great, Honored of the Worlds!"

The Lord Buddha enquired: "Would his mind and heart be correspondingly great, Subhuti? What is it that makes a man great? Is it the size of his body? Is it his unusual personality? Is it the work he accomplishes? Or is it the wisdom and compassion and selflessness of this behavior? Subhuti, what is behavior? There is no such thing; it is something the mind imagines, just like body and personality; it is only a name.

Then the Lord Buddha continued: "Nevertheless, if a good disciple, man or woman, studies this Scripture and thoughtfully observes even a verse of it, his merit will be very great. What words can express the merit of a disciple who, living with restraint and kindness, diligently studies and observes it! Such a disciple is attaining powers commensurate with the supreme and most wonderful Dharma. Wherever there is the hermitage of such a good disciple, it is the treasure-house of this sacred Scripture; it is a shrine of the Lord Buddha; and over it will hover uncounted Bodhisattvas of highest reverence and honor."

KSHANTI PARAMITA—IDEAL PATIENCE

At that time the Lord Buddha addressed Subhuti, saying: "If a good disciple, whether man or woman, devoted to the observance and study of this Scripture, is thereby lightly esteemed or despised, it is because, in a previous life there had been committed some grievous transgression, now followed by its inexorable retribution. But, although in this life lightly esteemed or despised, he bears it patiently, the compensating merit thus acquired will cause the transgression of a former life to be fully expiated, and the patient disciple will be adequately recompensed by his final attainment of supreme spiritual enlightenment."

(Regarding this Kshanti Paramita—Ideal Patience—it is said in the Sutra: "If disciples meet with the ills of life they should not shun them. If they suffer painful experiences, they should not feel afflicted or treated unjustly, but should always rejoice in remembering and contemplating the deep significance of the Dharma.')

The Lord Buddha continued: "Numberless ages ago, Subhuti, before the advent of Dipankara Buddha, there were many other Buddhas and I recall my difficult experiences while serving them and receiving their religious instruction and discipline, but I endured it patiently and, because my conduct was entirely blameless and without reproach, I was reborn in the days of Dipankara Buddha. But in the ages to come, if a disciple faithfully study and put into practice the teaching of this Scripture, the merit that he will thus acquire will far exceed the merit of my service in the days of those many Buddhas.

"In a previous life, Subhuti, when the Prince of Kalinga severed the flesh from my limbs and body, because of the discipline I had undergone in the past I remained patient, I was oblivious to such ideas as phenomena as an entity, a person, a living person, a personality. If I had not been oblivious to such ideas, when my limbs and body were torn apart, there would have originated in my mind feelings of anger and resentment. I recollect, five hundred incarnations ago, that I was practising this Kshanti Paramita and, because of it, I got rid of such arbitrary ideas. Therefore, Subhuti, an enlightened disciple ought to discard, as being unreal and illusive, every conceivable form of hindering phenomena.

Subhuti, in aspiring to supreme spiritual wisdom, the mind ought to be insensible to every sensuous influence, and be independent of everything pertaining to form, sound, odour, taste, touch, or discrimination. There ought to be cultivated a condition of complete independence of mind; because, if the mind is depending upon any external thing, it is cherishing a delusion; in reality, there is nothing external to the mind. Even the whole realm of sentient life is ephemeral and illusory. Therefore, in the exercise of this Paramita, the mind of an enlightened disciple ought to be unperturbed by any form of phenomena."

The Lord Buddha addressed Subhuti, saying: "If an enlightened disciple in the exercise of this Paramita was patient in the face of external difficulties and steadily studied and observed this Scripture; and another disciple, realising that within the meaning and purport of it, there could be no abstract individual existence—no suffering, no one to suffer, no one to attain supreme spiritual enlightenment—and yet patiently accepts it and continues to perfect himself in its virtue, this disciple will have a cumulative merit greater than the former. And why? Because, he is unaffected by any consideration of merit or reward."

Subhuti enquired of the Lord Buddha: "In what respect are enlightened disciples unaffected by merit or reward?"

The Lord Buddha replied: "Enlightened disciples, having patiently accepted the truth of egolessness, do not aspire for supreme enlightenment in any spirit of covetousness or acquisitiveness; they never think of merit and its commensurate reward. But the Tathagata, because of his perfect wisdom, knows of their patience and knows that for them there is reserved a cumulative merit that is immeasurable and illimitable."

VIRYA PARAMITA—IDEAL ZEAL

The Lord Buddha said to Subhuti: "If within this universe a good disciple heaped together the seven treasures forming many elevations as Mount Sumeru, and entirely bestowed these treasures on the Tathagata as a gift in his exercise of charity; and another disciple sacrificed his life as many times as there are grains of sand in the river Ganges, would such disciples accumulate great merit, Subhuti?"

Subhuti replied: "They would accumulate great merit, indeed, Blessed One."

The Lord Buddha continued: "If a good disciple were to select a single verse of this Scripture, faithfully observe and study it, and then zealously explain it to others, he would relatively accumulate a greater merit."

(Regarding this Virya Paramita—Ideal Zeal-the Sutra says: "In the practice of all good deeds, disciples should never indulge in indolence. They should recall all their great mental and physical sufferings that they have undergone in the past on account of having coveted worldly objects and comforts during former and which did not give the least nourishment to their physical lives. They should, therefore, in order to be emancipated in the future from these sufferings, be indefatigably zealous and never let even the thought of indolence arise in their minds; but steadily and persistently out of deep compassion endeavor to benefit all beings. They should dauntlessly, energetically, unintermittently, six watches, day and night, pay homage to all the Buddhas, make offerings to them, praise them, repent and confess to them, aspire to the most excellent knowledge, and make sincere vows of unselfish service. It is only, thereby, that they can root, out the hindrances and foster their root of merit.")

"Subhuti, if a disciple takes pleasure in a narrow and exclusive form of doctrine, or is attached to false ideas as to an entity, a being, a living being, a personality, he cannot receive with profit the instruction of this Scripture nor can he find delight in its study. This Scripture is intended for those who are entering upon the path, as well as for those who are attaining the highest planes of spiritual wisdom. If a disciple zealously observes, studies and widely disseminates the knowledge of this Scripture, for such an one there will be cumulative merit, immeasurable, incomparable, illimitable, inconceivable. All such disciples will be endowed with transcendent spiritual wisdom and enlightenment."

The Lord Buddha continued: "What think you? May an enlightened disciple ponder within himself, saying, 'I will create numerous Buddhist Kingdoms?'"

Subhuti replied: "No, Honored of the Worlds! And why? Because, such thoughts would be incompatible with the Virya Paramita, and kingdoms thus imagined would not, in reality, be Buddhist Kingdoms. Such a phrase as 'the creation of Buddhist Kingdoms,' is merely a figure of speech."

The Lord Buddha continued: "What think you, Subhuti? Do you imagine that the Tathagata reflects within himself, 'I will bring salvation to all beings'? Entertain no such delusive thought. And why? Because, in reality, there is no such dharma as 'salvation' for any one; and there is no such thing as a living being to whom 'salvation' can be brought. What is referred to as an entity, a being, a living being, a personality, is not so in reality—it is only so understood by ignorant and uneducated people."

The Lord Buddha enquired of Subhuti, saying: "May a disciple who has 'entered the stream' which bears on to Nirvana, thus moralise within himself: I have attained the fruits commensurate with the merits of one who has 'entered the stream'?"

Subhuti replied: "No, Honored of the Worlds! And why? Because, 'entered the stream' is simply a descriptive term. A disciple who avoids the seductions of form, sound, odour, taste, touch, and their discriminations, is merely called, 'one who has entered the stream.'"

The Lord Buddha again enquired of Subhuti, saying: "What think you? Is a bhikshu who is subject to only one more reincarnation, to muse within himself, 'I have obtained the fruits in agreement with the merits of "a once returner"?' "Subhuti replied, saying: "No, Honored of the Worlds! And why? Because, 'a once returner' is merely a descriptive title denoting only one more reincarnation; but, in reality, there is no such condition as 'only one more reincarnation.' 'A once returner' is merely a descriptive title."

The Lord Buddha once again enquired of Subhuti, saying: "What think you? May a bhikshu who has attained so high a degree of spiritual merit that he is never again to be reincarnated, may he thus reflect within himself, I have obtained the fruits which accord with the merits of one who is never to return to this world of life-and-death?" Subhuti replied, saying: "No, Honored of the Worlds! And why? Because, 'a never returner' is merely a designation, meaning, 'immunity from reincarnation'; but, in reality, there is no such condition, hence 'a never returner' is merely a convenient name."

The Lord Buddha yet again enquired of Subhuti, saying: "What think you? May a Bodhisattva who has attained to absolute tranquillity of mind thus meditate within himself: I have obtained the position of an Arhat?" Subhuti replied, saying: "No, Honored of the Worlds! And why? Because, in reality, there is no such condition synonymous with the term Arhat. If an Arhat thus meditates within himself, 'I have obtained the condition of an Arhat,' there would be the obvious occurrence to his mind of such arbitrary concepts as an entity, a being, a living being, a personality. When the Blessed One declared of me that in tranquillity of mind, observance of the Dharma and spiritual perception, I was preeminent among the disciples, I did not think within myself: 'I am free from desire, I am an Arhat.' Had I thought thus, the Blessed One would not have declared concerning me: 'Subhuti delights in the austerities of an Arhat.' It was because I was perfectly tranquil and oblivious to all conditions, that the Lord Buddha declared: 'Subhuti delights in the austerities practised by the Arhats.'"

The Lord Buddha added: "True, Subhuti! Enlightened disciples in the exercise of the Viya Paramita ought to maintain within themselves a pure and single mind; they should be unconscious of sensuous conditions and cultivate a mind that is independent of material circumstances. And why? Because, all sensuous conditions and material circumstances are only manifestations of mind and are alike dream-like and imaginary.

"Subhuti, A Bodhisattva should have a heart filled with compassion for all sentient life, but if he should think within his mind: 'I will deliver all beings,' he ought not to be called a Bodhisattva. And why? Because, in the first place, if there is no living being, no personality, then there is no one to be called a Bodhisattva. And in the second place, the Tathagata has declared: 'All beings are without self, without life, without personality.' Who then is to be delivered? If a Bodhisattva were to say: 'I will create many Buddha-lands,' he would say what is untrue. And why, Because, the idea of a Buddha-land is wholly imaginary, it is only a name.

"But O Subhuti, the Bodhisattva who believes that all things are without selfhood, and still has compassion and faith, he is, indeed, a noble minded Bodhisattva, and is so considered by the all-wise Tathagatas."

DHYANA PARAMITA—IDEAL TRANQUILLITY

Subhuti enquired of the Lord Buddha, saying: "Honored of the Worlds! In future ages, when this scripture is proclaimed amongst those beings destined to hear it, shall any conceive within their minds a sincere, unmingled faith?"

The Lord Buddha replied, saying: "Have no such apprehensive thought. Even at the remote period of five centuries subsequent to the Nirvana of the Tathagata, there will be many disciples observing the monastic vows and assiduously devoted to good works. These, hearing this Scripture proclaimed, will believe in its immutability and will conceive within their minds a pure, unmingled faith. Besides, it is important to realise that faith thus conceived, is not exclusively in virtue of the individual thought of any particular Buddha, but because of its affiliation with the universal thought of all the myriad Buddhas throughout the infinite ages. Therefore, among the beings destined to hear this Scripture proclaimed, many, by the Dhyana Paramita, will intuitively conceive a pure and holy faith.

"Subhuti, the Tathagata by his prescience is perfectly cognisant of all such potential disciples, and for these also there is reserved an immeasurable merit. And why? Because, the minds of these will not revert to such arbitrary concepts of phenomena as an entity, a being, a living being, a personality, having qualities or ideas coincident with the Dharma, or existing apart from the principle of the Dharma. And why? Because, assuming the permanency and reality of phenomena, the minds of these disciples would be involved in such distinctive ideas as an entity, a being, a living being, a personality. Affirming the permanency and reality of qualities or ideas coincident with the Dharma, their minds would inevitably be involved in resolving these same definitions. Postulating the inviolate nature of qualities or ideas which have an existence apart from the Dharma, there yet remains to be explained these abstruse distinctions—an entity, a being, a living being, a personality. Therefore, enlightened disciples ought not to affirm the permanency or reality of qualities or ideas coincident with the Dharma, nor postulate as being of an inviolate nature, qualities and ideas having an existence apart from the concept of the Dharma.

"Thus enlightened disciples are enabled to appreciate the significance of the words which the Tathagatas invariably repeat to their follows: 'Disciples must realise that the Dharma is presented to your minds in the simile of a raft.' If the Dharma—having fulfilled its function in bearing you to the other shore—must be abandoned together with all its coincident qualities and ideas, how much more inevitable must be the abandonment of qualities and ideas which have an existence apart from the Dharma?"

The Lord Buddha continued: "If a disciple had an amount of treasure sufficient to fill the illimitable universe and bestowed it upon the Tathagata in the exercise of charity, and if another disciple, having aspired to supreme spiritual wisdom, selected from this Scripture even a stanza of four lines only, observed it, diligently studied it and with zeal explained it to others, the cumulative merit of such a disciple would be relatively greater than the merit of the former. But, Subhuti, the attitude of his mind in which he explained it is important. It should be explained with a mind filled with compassion but free from any assumption as to the reality of an entity, a being, a living being, a personality, or as to the permanency or reality of earthly phenomena, or as to the validity of any ideas concerning them. And why? Because the phenomena of life are like a dream, a phantasm, a bubble, a shadow, the glistening dew, a lightning flash; thus should they be contemplated by an enlightened disciple. His mind should, at all times, be resting in the blessedness of tranquillity which invariably accompanies the practice of the Dhyana Paramita."

(Regarding the Dhyana Paramita—Ideal Tranquillity—the Sutra says: "The beginner should consider and practise Dhyana in two aspects: as cessation of the mind's intellectual activities, and as realisation of insight. To bring all mental states that produce vagrant thinking to a stand is called cessation. To adequately understand the transitory and emptiness and egolessness of all things is insight. At first each of them should be practised separately by the beginner, but when, by degrees, he attains facility, and finally attains perfection, the two aspects will naturally blend into one perfect state of mental tranquillity. Those who practise Dhyana should dwell in solitude and, sitting erect, should remain motionless, seeking to quiet the mind. Do not fix the thoughts on any definite thing that you have sensed or discriminated, or memorised; all particularisations, all imaginations, all recollections, are to be excluded, because all things are uncreate, devoid of all attributes, ever changing. In all thinking, something precedes that has been awakened by an external stimuli, so in Dhyana one should seek to abandon all notions connected with an external world. Then in thinking, something follows that has been elaborated in his own mind; so he should seek to abandon thinking. Because his attention is distracted by the external world, he is warned to turn to his inner, intuitive consciousness. If the process of mentation begins again, he is warned not to let his mind become attached to anything, because, independent of mind they have no existence. Dhyana is not at all to be confined to sitting erect in meditation; one's mind should be concentrated at all times, whether sitting, standing, moving, working; one should constantly discipline himself to that end. Gradually entering into the state of Samadhi, he will transcend all hindrances and become strengthened in faith, a faith that will be immovable.")

The Lord Buddha resumed his words to Subhuti, saying: "What think you, Subhuti, are the atoms of dust in the myriad worlds which comprise the universe, are they very numerous?"

Subhuti replied: "Very numerous, indeed, Blessed One."

The Lord Buddha continued: "Subhuti, these atoms of dust, many as they are, are not in reality 'atoms of dust,' they are merely termed so. Moreover, these 'myriad worlds' are not really worlds, they are merely termed so because of ignorance.

"Subhuti, if a good disciple were to take these infinite worlds and reduce them to exceedingly minute particles of dust and blow them away into space, would the so-called 'infinite worlds' cease to exist?"

Subhuti replied: "The Blessed One has already taught us that 'myriad worlds' is only a name; how can that which is only a name, cease to exist?"

Then the Lord Buddha continued: "True, Subhuti, but if it were otherwise, and the infinite worlds were a reality, then it would be asserting the unity and eternality of matter, which every one knows is dream-like, changing and transitory. Unity and eternality of matter, indeed! There is neither matter, nor unity, nor eternality—they are merely names. Belief in the unity and eternality of matter is incomprehensible; only common and worldly minded people, for purely materialistic reasons, cling to that hypothesis. Subhuti, enlightened disciples must thoroughly understand that emptiness and egolessness are characteristic of all Truth. The Dhyana Paramita can be successfully practised only from that viewpoint."

Then the Lord Buddha continued: "If a disciple should affirm that the Tathagata had enunciated a doctrine that the mind could comprehend the idea of an entity, a being, a living being, a personality, or ally other discrimination, would that disciple be interpreting aright the meaning of this Scripture?"

Subhuti replied: "Blessed One, that disciple would not be interpreting aright the meaning of the Lord Buddha's discourse. And why? Because, Blessed One, when you discoursed on belief in the reality of an entity, a being, a living being, a personality, it was plainly declared that there were no such things; that they were entirely unreal and illusive; that they were merely words."

The Lord Buddha continued: "Subhuti, the disciples who aspire to supreme spiritual wisdom ought thus to know, to believe in, and to interpret all phenomena. They ought to eliminate from their minds every seeming evidence of concrete objects; they ought to eliminate from their minds even the notions of such things; and become oblivious to every idea connected with them. And why? Because, so long as he cherishes ideas of and concerning an entity, a being, a living being, a personality, his mind is kept in confusion. He must even become oblivious to the idea that there is any one to whom the idea of sentient life can become oblivious. If he were to think within his mind, 'I must become oblivious to every idea of sentient life,' he could not be described as being wholly enlightened. And why? Because, within the bounds of reality there is no such thing, no entity, no being, no living being, no personality, nothing whatever that can be discriminated, and therefore, there can be no reality to ideas concerning them, for all these things are merely manifestations of the mind itself."

Subhuti enquired, saying: "Blessed One, in the ages to come, will sentient beings destined to hear this Dharma, awaken within their minds these essential elements of faith?"

The Lord Buddha replied, smiling: "Subhuti, it cannot be asserted that there are or will be any such things as sentient beings, nor can it be asserted that there will not be. At present there are none, they are merely termed 'sentient beings.' And as to any one being saved: how can there be one to find it by seeking, or to know it if it is ever found? One cannot gain self-realisation of Prajna Paramita without transcending the conscious faculty. To fully realise emptiness, egolessness, imagelessness by the use of the discriminating mind is futile. It is only by practising the Dhyana Paramita, by identifying oneself with emptiness and egolessness, that emptiness and egolessness is to be realised. In the exercise of the Dhyana Paramita, unless the mind of the enlightened disciple is independent of all phenomena, he is like a person lost in impenetrable darkness, to whom every object is invisible and himself helpless. But an enlightened disciple practising the Paramita with a mind independent of every phenomena, is like unto a person to whom suddenly the power of vision is restored, and he sees every thing as in the meridian glory of the sunlight."

The Lord Buddha said:

"Not by means of visible form, Not by audible sound, Is Buddha to be perceived; Only in the solitude and purity of Dhyana Is one to realise the blessedness of Buddha."

PRAJNA PARAMITA—IDEAL WISDOM

The Lord Buddha addressing Subhuti, said: "What think you? When in a previous life I was a disciple of Dipankara Buddha, did I eventually become a Buddha because of some prescribed teaching or system of doctrine?"

Subhuti replied: "No, Blessed One. When the Lord Buddha was a disciple of Dipankara Buddha neither prescribed teaching nor system of doctrine was communicated to him, whereby he eventually became a Buddha."

The Lord Buddha continued, saying: "In my discourses have I presented a system of doctrine that can be specifically formulated?"

Subhuti replied: "As I understand the meaning of the Blessed One's discourses, he has no system of doctrine that can be specifically formulated. And why? Because, what the Blessed One adumbrates in the terms of the Dharma is, in reality, inscrutable and inexpressible. Being a purely spiritual concept, it is neither consonant with the Dharma, nor synonymous with anything apart from the Dharma; but it is exemplified in the manner in which Bodhisattvas and holy Buddhas have regarded intuitive self-realisation as the highest law of their minds and by it have severally attained to different planes of spiritual wisdom."

The Lord Buddha endorsed these words, saying: "True it is; Subhuti! True it is. There is no dharma by means of which Buddhas attain supreme spiritual wisdom. Wisdom is attained only by self-realisation through the practice of the Dhyana Paramita. If there had been such a Dharma, Dipankara would not have prophesied when I was a disciple of his: 'In future ages, my boy, you will become Shakyamuni Buddha.' And why? Because in the concept *Buddha* every dharma is wholly and intelligibly comprehended. How could there be a Dharma by which that all-inclusive state could be attained? The supreme spiritual wisdom to which Buddhas attain, cannot, in its essence, be defined as either real or unreal. That which is commonly spoken of as the Buddha Dharma is synonymous with every moral and spiritual dharma. Subhuti, what are spoken of as 'systems of dharma,' including even the so-called Buddha Dharma, are not in reality systems of dharma, they are merely termed 'systems of dharma.'"

(Regarding the Prajna Paramita—Ideal Wisdom—really, there is no such thing. Prajna Paramita transcends all ideation, all knowledge, all wisdom; It is Noble Wisdom in its "suchness" and its self-nature is manifested in the transformation-bodies of the Tathagatas.)

Subhuti enquired of the Lord Buddha: "In attaining supreme spiritual wisdom did the Lord Buddha, then, attain nothing definite and tangible?"
The Lord Buddha replied: "In attaining supreme spiritual wisdom, not a vestiage of dharma nor doctrine was obtained, that is why it is called 'supreme spiritual wisdom.' Prajna Paramita is universal, coherent, indivisible; it is neither above nor below; it excludes all such arbitrary ideas as an entity, a being, a living being, a personality, discrimination, ideation; but it includes every dharma pertaining to the cultivation of wisdom and compassion. And even these, when defined and thought about, are not in reality 'dharmas of wisdom and compassion'; they are only termed 'dharmas of wisdom and compassion.'

"Do not think that the Tathagatas consider within themselves: 'I ought to promulgate a system of Dharma.' Have no such irrelevant thought, Subhuti. and why? because by so thinking the disciple would expose his ignorance and defame the Tathagatas. In reality there is no 'system of Dharma' to promulgate; it is only termed 'a system of Dharma.'

"What think you? Can the Tathagatas be perceived by their perfect material bodies, or by any physical phenomena?"

Subhuti replied: "It is improbable that a Lord Buddha can be perceived by his perfect material body, or by any physical phenomena; because, in reality, there is no such thing as a material body, nor physical phenomena; they are only terms that are in common use."

Then the Lord Buddha said: "Why is the Tathagata so named? It is because he manifests the essential nature of reality. 'He who thus comes,' comes from nowhere. He symbolises the emptiness of qualities, the egolessness, the imagelessness, of ultimate reality. He symbolises the un-born, the un-originate, the truly eternal because the ultimate. And yet, Subhuti, if any one should affirm that by the Tathagata ultimate Wisdom is manifested, he would speak an untruth, he would slander me by his limited knowledge. That which is manifested by the Tathagatas is neither truth nor falsehood: it is no-thing-ness; and yet it is inconceivable Oneness, because it is Prajna Paramita, because it is the essence nature of Buddahood.

"Subhuti, the plane of thought to which the Buddhas attain and which the Tathagatas manifest, cannot be expressed in terms of reality or in terms of non-reality. Their utterances are neither extravagant nor chimerical; they are true, credible, immutable, but can never be expressed in the limits of words and doctrines.

Then the Lord Buddha enquired of Subhuti, saying: "Are Tathagatas to be recognised by the works they do and the effects they produce?"
Subhuti replied: "No, Blessed One; a Buddha is not to be known by his works, else would a great world-conquering King be a Buddha."
The Lord Buddha said: "Just so, Subhuti. It is not by a great show of erudition, nor by the building of anything, nor by the destruction of anything, that the Tathagatas are to be known. It is only within the deepest consciousness of Bodhisattvas through the self-realisation of the Prajna Paramita, that the Tathagatas are to be realised.
The Lord Buddha continued: "What think you, Subhuti? Does the Tathagata possess a physical eye?" Subhuti assented, saying: "The Blessed One truly possesses a physical eye."

"What think you, Subhuti? Does the Tathagata possess the eye of enlightenment?" Subhuti assented, saying: "The Blessed One truly possesses the eye of enlightenment."

"What think you, Subhuti? Does the Tathagata possess the eye of Wisdom?" Subhuti assented, saying: "The Blessed One truly possesses the eye of Wisdom."

"What think you, Subhuti? Does the Tathagata possess the eye of Compassion?" Subhuti assented, saying: "The Blessed One truly possesses the Buddha eye of Compassion."

The Lord Buddha continued: "If there were as many river Ganges as there are grains of sand in the river Ganges, and if there were as many Buddha-lands as there are grains of sand in all the innumerable rivers, would these Buddha-lands be numerous?"
Subhuti replied: "Buddha-lands are innumerable."
The Lord Buddha continued: "Subhuti, within these innumerable worlds are every form of sentient life with all their various mental capacities, dispositions, and temperaments, all alike are fully known to the Tathagatas, and the Tathagatas are filled with compassion for them. Nevertheless, what are referred to as mental capacities, dispositions, and temperaments, are not in reality mental capacities, dispositions and temperaments; they are merely termed such. Dispositions of mind, modes of thought, whether relating to the past, present or future, are all alike unreal and illusory.

"Thus should the Noble Prajna Paramita be explained. Thus should a young disciple, whether man or woman, thus should the highest Bodhisattva, understand and explain the Prajna Paramita. Everything should be seen as solitude, as egoless, as imageless; everything should be seen as the sky, as sunlight, as darkness, as a phantom, as a dream, as a flash of lightning, as a bubble. Thus is Prajna Paramita to be conceived and to be explained."

Then the venerable Subhuti, hearing the text of this sacred Scripture expounded by the Lord Buddha, and realising its profound meaning, was moved to tears and, addressing the Lord Buddha, said: "Thou art of transcendent wisdom, Blessed One! In thus expounding this supreme Scripture, thou hast surpassed every exposition previously given. True it is that all things and all phenomena and all definitive ideas are transitory, empty, egoless, imageless and dream-like! Only Prajna Paramita abides."

The Lord Buddha assenting, said: "Subhuti, in future ages, disciples destined to hear this Scripture, discarding every arbitrary idea, neither becoming perturbed by its extreme mode of thought, nor carried away by its lofty sentiment, nor fearful as to realising its noble sentiment, who faithfully and zealously study it, observe its precepts, and patiently explain it to others, their intrinsic merits will excite superlative wonder and praise. Moreover, as they gain in realisation of this profound Prajna Paramita through the practice of Dhyana, they will eventually become wholly enlightened, wholly compassionate—themselves revealed as Buddha."

Subhuti enquired of the Lord Buddha: "Blessed One, by what name shall this Scripture be known, that we may regard it with reverence?"

The Lord Buddha replied: "Subhuti, this Scripture shall be known as THE DIAMOND SCRIPTURE, because, by its Transcendent Wisdom all sentient life shall reach the other shore. By this name you shall reverently regard it, always remembering that what is referred to as Transcendental Wisdom is only a name,—Prajna Paramita transcends all wisdom."

Sutra of Transcendental Wisdom

Based on Max Muller's Translation
Edited and Interpreted

Preface

THIS SUTRA, under the title of MAHA-PRAJNA-PARAMITA-HRIDAYA, formed another section of the great MAHA-PRAJNA-PARAMITA SUTRA. It is the shortest of all the great Sutras and on that account was memorised by all Buddhist monks and recited as part of the daily ritual, often many times a day. It is no wonder that its teaching of "emptiness" entered into the warp and woof of their thinking. In spite of the singleness of its teaching, it will repay a lifetime of thoughtful meditation.

Sutra of Transcendental Wisdom
(Maha-prajna-paramita-hridaya)

THUS HAVE I HEARD. At one time the Blessed One together with a number of the highest Bodhisattvas and a great company of bhikshus was staying at Rajagriha on Mount Gridhrakta.

The Blessed One was sitting apart absorbed in Samadhi, and the noble Bodhisattva Avalokitesvara was meditating on the profound Prajna-paramita, thinking thus: Personality is made up of five grasping aggregates--form, sensation, perception, discrimination and consciousness--all of which the Blessed One has taught us are by nature dream-like and empty.

Then the venerable Sariputra, influenced by the power of the Blessed One absorbed in Samadhi, spoke thus to the noble Bodhisattva Avalokitesvara: "If a son or daughter of good family wishes to study the profound Prajna-paramita, how is he to do so?"

The noble Bodhisattva Avalokitesvara replied to the venerable Sariputra: "If a son or daughter wishes to study the profound Prajna-paramita, he must think thus: Personality? What is personality? Is it an eternal entity or is it made up of elements that pass away?

"Personality is made up of five grasping aggregates which are by nature empty of any self-substance. Form, or matter, is emptiness; emptiness is not different from form, nor is form different from emptiness; indeed, emptiness is form. In like manner: sensation is emptiness; emptiness is not different from sensation, nor is sensation different from emptiness; indeed, emptiness is sensation. In like manner: perception, discrimination and consciousness are also emptiness.

"Thus, O Sariputra, all things having the character of emptiness, have no beginning nor ending; they are neither faultless nor not faultless; they are neither perfect nor imperfect. Therefore, in emptiness there is no form, no sensation, no perception, no discrimination, no consciousness. There is no eye, no ear, no nose, no tongue, no sensitiveness to contact, no mind. There is no form, no sound, no smell, no taste, no touch, no mental process, no object, no knowledge, no ignorance. There is no destruction of objects, no cessation of knowledge, no cessation of ignorance. There is no decay and no death, nor is there any destruction of the notions of decay and death. There is no Noble Fourfold Truth--no pain, no cause of pain, no cessation of pain, nor any Noble Path to the cessation of pain. There is no knowledge of Nirvana, there is no obtaining of Nirvana, there is no not-obtaining of Nirvana.

"Why is there no such thing as the obtaining of Nirvana? Because Nirvana is the realm of no-thing-ness. If the ego-soul of personality is an eternal entity it cannot attain Nirvana. It is only because personality is made up of elements and is, therefore, empty of an ego-soul, that it may attain Nirvana. So long as man is approaching Ultimate Wisdom, he is still dwelling in the realm of consciousness. If he is to realise Nirvana, he must pass beyond the realm of consciousness. In highest Samadhi when consciousness has been transcended, he has passed beyond discrimination and knowledge, beyond any reach of change or fear. He is already enjoying Nirvana.

"The perfect understanding of this and the patient acceptance of it is the Ultimate Wisdom that is Prajna-paramita. All the Buddhas of the past, present and future, having attained highest Samadhi, awake to find themselves realising this highest perfect Wisdom.

"Therefore, every one should seek self-realisation of Prajna-paramita, the Truth of Perfect Wisdom, the unsurpassable Truth, the Truth that ends all pain, the Truth that is forever True. O Prajna-paramita! O Transcendent Truth that spans the troubled ocean of life-and-death, safely carry all seekers to that other shore. Thus, O Sariputra, should a Bodhisattva teach all seekers the profound Prajna-paramita."

When the Blessed One had risen from Samadhi, he gave approval to the words of the noble Bodhisattva Avalokitesvara, saying: "Well done! Well done, Noble Son! So, indeed, must the study of the profound Prajna-paramita be presented. As it has been described by thee, it is approved by all the Tathagatas."

Thus spoke the Blessed One with joyful mind, and the noble Bodhisattva Avalokitesvara and the venerable Sariputra and the whole company of bhikshus praised the words of the Blessed One.

Sutra of
The Sixth Patrich

Based Upon Wong Mou-lam's Translation,
Edited and Interpreted

Preface

THIS VERSION is based upon the English translation entitled: SUTRA SPOKEN BY THE SIXTH PATRIARCH, WEI LANG, ON THE HIGH SEAT OF THE GEM OF LAW made by Mr. Wong Mou-lam of Shanghai, and published by the Yu Ching Press. To Mr. Wong great praise and credit should be given for his most excellent reproduction of the meaning and spirit of the original. Mr. Wong has very graciously given the editor permission to make changes in its English dress, and to delete passages that a reasonable amount of literary and historical criticism appear to make necessary, or that are of slight interest to our times. As Mr. Wong is in far away Ceylon to better fit himself for further translation work, there has been no chance to talk over the changes with him and to secure his approval; the editor, therefore, holds himself wholly responsible for them. Mr. Wong's translation is technically more complete and accurate and for scholarly research is to be preferred to this Version, but there is great need for a simpler and more readable Version, for which need this was provided.

The Sixth Chinese Patriarch lived fifteen hundred years ago (637-713), but his kindly and straight-forward insistence on the one thing: "Self-realisation of your own mind-essence," places him among the world's great teachers, and marks him out as one still worthy of attention.

Chapter I

Autobiography of Hui-Neng

ONCE WHEN THE PATRIARCH had come to Pao-lam Monastery, Prefect Wai of Shiu-chow and other officials came there to invite him to deliver public lectures on Buddhism in the hall of Tai-fan Temple in the city (Canton).

When the time came, there were assembled Prefect Wai, government officials and Confucian scholars about thirty each, bhikshu, bhikshuni, Taoists and laymen, nearly a thousand in all. After the Patriarch had taken his seat, the congregation in a body paid him homage and asked him to speak on the fundamental truths of Buddhism. Whereupon, His Eminence delivered the following address:—

Learned Audience, our self-nature which is the seed or kernel of Bodhi (the Wisdom that comes with enlightenment) is pure by nature and by making right use of it we can reach Buddhahood directly. Let me tell you something about my own life and how I came into possession of this inner teaching of our Ch'an School.

My father, a native of Fan-yang, was dismissed from his official post and banished to become a commoner in Sun-chow in Kwang-tung. My father died when I was quite young leaving my mother poor and miserable, to my great misfortune. We moved to Kwang-chow (now Canton) and lived in very bad circumstances. I was selling firewood in the market one day when one of my customers ordered some to be sent to his shop. Upon delivery and payment for the same as I went outside I found a man reciting a Sutra. No sooner had I heard the text of this Sutra then my mind became at once enlightened. I asked the man the name of the book he was reciting and was told that it was the "Diamond Sutra" (*Vajrakkhedika*). I asked him where he came from and why he recited this particular Sutra. He replied that he came from the Tung-tsan Monastery in the Wong-mui District of Kee-chow; that the Abbot in charge of this temple was Hwang-yan who was the Fifth Patriarch and had about a thousand disciples under him; and that when he went there to pay homage to the Patriarch, he found him lecturing on this Diamond Sutra. He further told me that his Eminence was in the habit of encouraging the laity as well as his monks to recite this scripture, as by so doing they might realise their own essence-of-mind and thereby reach Buddhahood directly.

It must be due to my good karma accumulated from past lives that I heard about this and that later on I was given ten taels for the maintenance of my mother by a man who advised me to go to Wong-mui to interview the Fifth Patriarch. After arrangements had been made for my mother's support, I left for Wong-mui which took me about thirty days to reach.

I paid homage to the Patriarch and was asked where I came from and what I expected to get from him. I replied that I was a commoner from Sunchow in Kwang-tung and had travelled far to pay my respects to him, and then said, "I ask for nothing but Buddhahood."

The Patriarch replied: "So you are a native of Kwang-tung, are you? You evidently belong to the aborigines; how can you expect to become a Buddha?"

I replied: "Although there are Northern men and Southern men, but North or South make no difference in their Buddha-nature. An aboriginee is different from your Eminence physically, but there is no difference in our Buddha-nature."

He was going to speak further to me but the presence of other disciples made him hesitate and he told me to join the other laborers at their tasks. "May I tell Your Eminence," I urged, "that Prajna (transcendental Wisdom) constantly rises in my mind. As one cannot go astray from his own nature one may be rightly called, 'a field of merit' (this is a title of honor given to monks as a monk affords the best of opportunities to others, 'to sow the seed of merit'). I do not know what work Your Eminence would ask me to do."

"This aboriginee is very witty" he remarked. "Go to the work-rooms and say no more." I then withdrew to the rear where the work of the monastery was carried on and was told by a lay brother to split firewood and hull rice.

More than eight months after the Patriarch met me one day and said, "I know that your knowledge of Buddhism is very sound, but I have to refrain from speaking with you lest evil men should harm you. Do you understand?" "Yes Sir, I understand," I replied. "And I will not go near your hall, lest people take notice of me."

One day the Patriarch assembled all his disciples and said to them: "The question of incessant rebirth is a very momentous one, but instead of trying to free yourselves from that bitter sea of life and death, you men, day after day, seem to be going after tainted merits only. Merit will be of no help to you if your essence of mind is polluted and clouded. Go now and seek for the transcendental wisdom that is within your own minds and then write me a stanza about it. He who gets the clearest idea of what Mind-essence is will be given the insignia of the Patriarch; I will give him the secret teaching of the Dharma, and will appoint him to be the Sixth Patriarch. Go away quickly, now, and do not delay in writing the stanza; deliberation is quite unnecessary and will be of no use. The one who has realised Essence of Mind can testify to it at once as soon as he is spoken to about it. He cannot lose sight of it, even if he were engaged in a battle."

Having received this instruction, the disciples withdrew and said to one another, "There is no use of our making an effort to write a stanza and submit it to His Eminence; the Patriarchship is bound to go to Elder Shinshau, our Master, anyway. Why go through the form of writing, it will only be a waste of energy." Hearing this they decided to write nothing, saying,

"Why should we take the trouble to do it? Hereafter we will simply follow our Master Shin-shau wherever he goes and will look to him for guidance."

Shin-shau reasoned within himself, "Considering that I am their Master, none of them will take part in competition. I wonder whether I should write a stanza and submit it to His Eminence, or not. If I do not, how can the Patriarch know how deep or how superficial my knowledge is? If my object is to get the Dharma, my motive is pure. If it is to get the Patriarchship, then it is bad; my mind would be that of a worldling and my action would amount to a theft of the Patriarch's holy seat. But if I do not submit the stanza, I will lose my chance of getting the Dharma. It is very difficult to know what to do."

In front of the Patriarch's hall there were three corridors the walls of which were to be painted by a court artist named Lo-chun, with pictures suggested by the Lankavatara Sutra depicting the transfiguration of the assembly, and with scenes showing the genealogy of the five Patriarchs, for the information and veneration of the public. When Shin-shau had composed his stanza he made several attempts to submit it, but his mind was so perturbed that he was prevented from doing it. Then he suggested to himself, "It would be better for me to write it on the wall of the corridor and let the Patriarch find it himself. If he approves it, then I will go to pay him homage and tell him that it was done by me; but if he disapproves it,—well, then I have wasted several years' time in this mountain receiving homage which I did not deserve. If I fail, what progress have I made in learning Buddhism?"

At midnight of that night, he went secretly to write his stanza on the wall of the south corridor, so that the Patriarch might know to what spiritual insight he had attained. The stanza read:—

"Our body may be compared to the Bodhi-tree; While our mind is a mirror bright. Carefully we cleanse and watch them hour by hour, And let no dust collect upon them."

As soon as he had written it he returned at once to his room, so no one knew what he had done. In the quiet of his room he pondered: "When the Patriarch sees my stanza tomorrow, if he is pleased with it it will show that I am (spiritually) ready for the Dharma; but if he disapproves of it, then it will mean that I am unfit for the Dharma owing to misdeeds in previous lives and karmic accumulations that so thickly becloud my mind. What will the Patriarch say about it? How difficult it is to speculate." He could neither sleep nor sit at ease; and so in this vein he kept on thinking until dawn.

In the morning the Patriarch sent for Lo, the court artist, to have the walls painted with pictures and went with him to the south corridor. The Patriarch noticed the stanza and said to the artist, "I am sorry to have troubled you to come so far, but the walls do not need to be painted now. The Sutra says, 'All forms and phenomena are transient and illusive'; we will leave the stanza here so that people may study the stanza and recite it. If they put its teachings into actual practice, they will be saved from the misery of being born in evil realms of existence. Any one who practices it will gain great merit." The Patriarch ordered incense to be burnt before it, and instructed all his disciples to pay homage to it and to recite it, so that they might realise Essence of Mind. After his disciples had recited it, they all exclaimed, "Well done!"

That midnight the Patriarch sent for Shin-shau and asked if he had written the stanza. Shin-shau admitted that he had written it and then added: "I am not so vain as to expect to get the Patriarchship, but I wish Your Eminence would kindly tell me whether my stanza shows the least grain of wisdom."

"To attain supreme enlightenment," replied the Patriarch, "one must be able to know spontaneously one's own self-nature which is neither created nor can it be annihilated. From one momentary sensation to another, one should always be able to realise Essence of Mind; then all things will be free from restraint. Once the self-nature of Mind-essence is realised, forever after one will be free from delusion, and under all circumstances, one's mind will remain in a state of 'Suchness' (*tathata*). Such a state of mind is absolute truth. If you can see things in such a state of mind you have realised Essence of Mind, which is the supreme enlightenment. You had better return now and think it over for a couple of days and then submit another stanza. In case the new stanza shows that you have entered 'the door of enlightenment,' I will transmit to you the robe and the Dharma."

Shin-shau made obeisance to the Patriarch and went away. For several days he tried in vain to write another stanza, which upset his mind so much that he was as ill at ease as though he was in a nightmare; he could find comfort neither in sitting nor walking.

Two days after, it happened that a boy who was passing by the room where I was hulling rice, was loudly reciting the stanza written by Shin-shau. As soon as I heard it I knew at once that its composer had not yet realised Essence of Mind. Although at that time I never had had instruction about it, I already had a general idea of it. "What stanza is this," I asked the boy. "You aboriginee," he said, "don't you know about it? The Patriarch told his disciples that the question of rebirth was a momentous one, and those who wished to inherit his robe and the Dharma should write him a stanza and the one who had the true idea of Mind-essence would get them and become the Sixth Patriarch. Elder Shin-shau wrote this 'formless' stanza on the wall of the south corridor and the Patriarch told us to recite it. He also said that those who put its teachings into actual practice would attain great merit and be saved from being born in the evil realms of existence."

I told the boy that I wished to learn the stanza also, so that I might have the benefit of it in future life. Although I had been hulling rice for eight months, I had never been to the hall, so I asked the boy to show me where the stanza was written, so that I might make obeisance to it. The boy took me there and as I was illiterate, I asked him to read it to me. A petty officer of the Kong-chow District, named Chang Fat-yung, who happened to be there, then read it clearly. When he had finished reading, I told him that I, also, had composed a stanza and asked him to write it for me. "Extraordinary," he exclaimed, "that you, also, can compose a stanza."

"If you are a seeker of supreme enlightenment, you will not despise a beginner," I said.

"Please recite your stanza," said he, "I will write it down for you, but if you should succeed in getting the Dharma, do not forget to deliver me."

My stanza read as follows:

"Neither is there Bohi-tree, Nor case of mirror bright. Since intrinsically all is void Where can dust collect?"

Later on seeing that a crowd was collecting, the Patriarch came out and erased the stanza with his shoe lest jealous ones should do me injury. Judging by this, the crowd took it for granted that the author of it had also not yet realised Mind-essence.

Next day the Patriarch came secretly to the room where the rice was being hulled and seeing me at work with the stone pestle, said, "A seeker of the Path risks his life for the Dharma. Should he do so?" Then he asked, "Is the rice ready?" "Ready long ago," I replied, "only waiting for the sieve." He knocked the mortar thrice with his stick and went away.

Knowing what his signal meant, in the third watch of the night, I went to his room. Using his robe as a screen so that no one would see us, he expounded the Diamond Sutra to me. When he came to the sentence, "One should use one's mind in such a way that it will be free from any attachment," I suddenly became thoroughly enlightened and realised that all things in the universe are Mind-essence itself.

1 said to the Patriarch, "Who could have conceived that Mind-essence is intrinsically pure! Who could have conceived that Mind-essence is intrinsically free from becoming and annihilation! That Mind-essence is intrinsically self-sufficient, and free from change! Who could have conceived that all things are manifestations of Mind-essence!"

Thus at midnight, to the knowledge of no one, was the Dharma transmitted to me, and I consequently became the inheritor of the teachings of the "Sudden" School, and the possessor of the robe and the begging-bowl.

"You are now the Sixth Patriarch," said His Eminence. "Take good care of yourself and deliver as many sentient beings as possible. Spread the teaching; keep the teaching alive; do not let it come to an end. Listen to my stanza:

'*Sentient beings who sow seed of Enlightenment In the field of causation, will reap the fruit of Buddhahood. Inanimate objects which are void of Buddha-nature Sow not and reap not.*'"

His Eminence further said: "When Patriarch Bodhidharma first came to China, few Chinese had confidence in him and so this robe has been handed down as a testimony from one Patriarch to another. As to the Dharma, as a rule it is transmitted from heart to heart and the recipient is expected to understand it and to realise it by his own efforts. From time immemorial, it has been the practice for one Buddha to pass on to his successor the quintessence of the Dharma, and for one Patriarch to transmit to another, from mind to mind, the esoteric teaching. As the robe may give cause for dispute, you will be the last one to inherit it. If you should again hand it down to a successor, your life would be in imminent danger. You must now leave this place as quickly as you can, lest some one should harm you."

I asked him, "Where shall I go?" and he replied, "Stop at Wei and seclude yourself at Wui."

As it was the middle of the night when I thus received the begging-bowl and the robe, I told the Patriarch that as I was a Southerner I did not know the mountain trails and it would be impossible for me to get down to the river. "You need not worry," he replied, "I will go with you." He then accompanied me to the Kiu-kiang landing where we got a boat. As he started to do the rowing himself, I asked him to be seated and let me handle the oar. He replied, "It is only right for me to get you across." (This is an illusion to the sea of birth and death which one has to cross before the shore of Nirvana can be reached.) To this I replied, "(So long as I was) under illusion, I was dependent on you to get me across, but now it is different. It was my fortune to be born on the frontier and my education is very deficient, but I have had the honor to inherit the Dharma from you; since I am now enlightened, it is only right for me to cross the sea of birth and death by my own effort to realise my own Essence of Mind."

"Quite so, quite so," he agreed. "Beginning with you (Ch'an) Buddhism will become very widespread. Three years from your leaving me I shall pass from this world. You may start on your journey now; go as fast as you can toward the South. Do not begin preaching too soon; (Ch'an) Buddhism is not to be easily spread."

After saying good-bye, I left him and walked toward the South. In about two months I reached the Tai-yu Mountain where I noticed several hundred men were in pursuit of me with the intention of recovering the robe and begging-bowl. Among them, the most vigilant was a monk of the name of Wei-ming whose surname was Chen. In lay-life he had been a general of the fourth rank. His manner was rough and his temper hot. When he overtook me, I threw the robe and the begging-bowl on a rock, saying, "This robe is nothing but a testimonial; what is the use of taking it away by force?" When he reached the rock, he tried to pick them up but could not. Then in astonishment he shouted, "Lay Brother, Lay Brother, (Hui-neng, although appointed the Sixth Patriarch, had not yet formally been admitted to the Order), I have come for the Dharma; I do not care for the robe." Whereupon I came from my hiding place and took the position on the rock of a Patriarch. He made obeisance and said, "Lay Brother, I beg you to teach me."

"Since the object of your coming is for the Dharma," said I, "please refrain from thinking about anything and try to keep your mind perfectly empty and receptive. I will then teach you." When he had done this for a considerable time, I said, "Venerable Sir, at the particular moment when you are thinking of neither good nor evil, what is your real self-nature (the word is, physiognomy)?"

As soon as he heard this he at once become enlightened, but he asked, "Apart from these sayings and ideas handed down by the Patriarchs from generation to generation, are there still any esoteric teachings?"

"What I can tell you is not esoteric," I replied, "If you turn your light inward, you will find what is esoteric within your own mind."

"In spite of my stay in Wong-mui," said he, "I did not realise my own self-nature. Now, thanks to your guidance, I realise it in the same way a water-drinker knows how hot and how cold the water is. Lay Brother, I am now your disciple." I replied, "If this is the case, then you and I are fellow disciples of the Fifth Patriarch. Please take good care of yourself." He paid homage and departed.

Some time after I reached Tso-kai, but as evil-doers were again persecuting me, I took refuge in Sze-wui where I staid with a party of hunters for fifteen years. They used to put me to watch their nets, but when I found living creatures entangled in them I would set them free. At meal time I would put vegetables in the same pan in which they cooked their meat. Some of them questioned me and I explained to them that I could only eat vegetables. Occasionally I talked to them in a way that befitted their understanding. One day I bethought myself that I ought not to pass so secluded a life all the time; I felt that the time had come for me to propagate the Dharma. Accordingly I left there and went to the Fat-shin Temple in Canton.

At the time I reached that temple, the monk Yen-chung, Master of Dharma, was lecturing on the Maha Parinirvana Sutra. It happened one day when a pennant was being blown about by the wind, that two monks entered into a dispute as to what was in motion, the wind or the pennant. As they failed to settle their difference, I suggested that it was neither; that what actually moved was their own mind. The whole group was surprised by what I said and the Master Yen-chung invited me to a seat of honor and questioned me about various knotty points in the Sutra. Seeing that my answers were precise and accurate, that they inferred more than book knowledge, he said to me, "Lay Brother, you must be an extraordinary man. I was told long ago that the inheritor of the Fifth Patriarch's robe and Dharma had come to the South; very likely you are the man?"

To this I politely assented. He made obeisance and courteously asked me to show to the assembly the robe and begging-bowl which I had inherited. He further asked what instructions I had received at the time the Fifth Patriarch had transmitted the Dharma to me. I replied, "Apart from a discussion on the realisation of Mind-essence, he gave me no other instruction. He did not refer to Dhyana nor to Emancipation." The Master asked, "Why not?" I replied, "Because that would mean there were two ways in Buddhism. There cannot be two ways; in Buddhism there is only one way." The Master then asked, "What is the only way?" I replied, "The Maha Parinirvana Sutra which you are expounding teaches that Buddha-nature is the only way. For example: in that Sutra King-ko-kwai-tak, a Bodhisattva, asked the Buddha whether those who commit the four serious sins, or the five deadly sins, or are heretics, etc., would thereby root out their 'element of goodness' and their Buddha-nature. Buddha replied, 'There are two kinds of 'goodness-elements': an eternal element, and a non-eternal. Since Buddha-nature is neither eternal nor non-eternal, their 'element of goodness' is not eradicated. There are good ways and evil ways, but since Buddha-nature is neither good nor evil, Buddhism is known as having no two ways. From the point of view of ordinary folks, the component parts of a personality and the factors of consciousness are two separate aggregates, but enlightened men know and understand that they are not dual in nature. It is that nature of non-duality that is Buddha-nature."

Master Yen-chung was pleased with my answer. Putting his hands together in token of respect, he said, "My interpretation of the Sutra is as worthless as a heap of debris, while your discourse is as valuable as pure gold." Subsequently he conducted a ceremony of initiation, receiving me into the order, and then asked me to accept him as a pupil.

Thenceforth under the Bodhi-tree I have discoursed about the teachings of the Fourth and Fifth Patriarchs. Since the Dharma was transmitted to me in Tung Mountain, I have gone through many hardships and often my life seemed to be hanging by a thread. Today I have had the honor of meeting Your Highness, and you, officials, monks and nuns, Taoists and laymen, in this great assembly. I must ascribe this good fortune to our happy connection in previous kalpas, as well as to our common accumulated merits in making offerings to various Buddhas in our past incarnations. Otherwise we would have had no chance of hearing the teachings of the "Sudden" School of Ch'an and thereby laying the foundation of our present success in understanding the Dharma.

This teaching is not a system of my own invention, but has been handed down by the Patriarchs. Those who wish to hear the teaching should first purify their own minds; and after hearing it, each must clear up his own doubts, even as the Sages have done in the past.

At the end of the address, the assembly felt rejoiced, made obeidance and departed.

Chapter II

Discourse on Prajna

ON THE FOLLOWING DAY Prefect Wai asked Patriarch to give another address. Having taken his seat, the Patriarch asked the assembly to first purify their minds (by a period of dhyana-silence) and then to join in reciting the Maha Prajna-paramita Sutra, after which he gave the following address:—

Learned Audience: Prajna, the Wisdom of Enlightenment, is inherent in every one of us. It is because of the delusions under which our minds labor that we fail to realise its presence, and that we have to seek the advice and the guidance of the more highly enlightened before we can realise it in our mind's Essence. You should know that as far as Buddha-nature is concerned, there is no difference between an enlightened man and an ignorant one. What makes the difference is that one realises it and the other is ignorant of it. Let me speak to you now about the Maha Prajna-paramita Sutra, so that each of you may attain wisdom. Listen carefully while I speak.

Learned Audience: There are many people who recite the word, Prajna, the whole day long, who do not seem to know that Prajna is inherent in their own nature. The mere talking about food will not appease hunger, but that is the very thing these people are doing. We may talk about the "Doctrine of Voidness" for myriads of kalpas, but merely talking about it will not enable one to realise it in his Mind-essence, and the talking will serve no good purpose in the end.

The name, Maha Prajna-paramita, is Sanskrit and means, "great Wisdom to reach the opposite shore." Now, what we ought to do with it is to carry it into practice with our mind; whether we recite it or do not recite it matters little. Mere reciting without mental practice, may be likened to a phantasm, a magical delusion, a flash of lighting, or a dew-drop. On the other hand, if we do both, then our mind will be in accord with what we repeat orally. Our very self-nature is Buddha, and apart from this nature there is no other Buddha.

What is Maha? Maha means, "great." The capacity of the mind is as great as that of space. It is infinite, it is neither round nor square, neither great nor small, neither green nor yellow, neither red nor white, neither above nor below, neither long nor short, neither angry nor happy, neither right nor wrong, neither good nor evil, neither first nor last. All Buddha-lands are as void as space. Intrinsically our transcendental nature is void and not a single dharma can be attained. It is the same with Mind-essence which is a state of the "voidness of non-voidity."

Learned Audience: when you hear me speak about the void, do not fall into the idea that I mean vacuity. It is of the utmost importance that we should not fall into that idea, because then when a man sits quietly and keeps his mind blank he would be abiding in a state of the "voidness of indifference." The illimitable void of the Universe its capable of holding myriads of things of various shapes and form, such as the sun and the moon, and the stars, worlds, mountains, rivers, rivulets, springs, woods, bushes, good men, bad men, laws pertaining to goodness and to badness, heavenly planes and hells, great oceans and all the mountains of Mahameru. Space takes in all these, and so does the voidness of our nature. We say that Essence of Mind is great because it embraces all things since all things are within our nature. When we see the goodness or the badness of other people, and are not attracted by it, nor repulsed by it, nor attached to it, then the attitude of our mind is as void as space. In that we see the greatness of our minds, therefore we call Mind-essence, Maha.

Learned Audience: When ignorant people have ideas they merely talk about them, but wise men keep them within their own minds and put them into practice. There is also a class of foolish people who sit quietly and try to keep their minds blank; they refrain from thinking of anything and then call themselves "great." Concerning this heretical view, I have no patience to speak. You should know that the capacity of the mind is very great since it pervades the whole Universe wherever the domain of Law extends. When we use the mind we can consider everything; when we use Mind to its full capacity, we shall know all. All under one principle, one principle in all. When Mind works without hindrance and is at perfect liberty to come" or to "go," then Mind is Prajna.

Prajna comes from Mind-essence and not from any exterior source. Do not have any mistaken notion about that. To cherish mistaken notions about that is to make a "selfish use of True Nature." Once the "True Nature" of Mind-essence is realised, one will be forever free from delusion. Since the capacity of Mind is for great things, we should not busy it with trivial acts. (That is, the mind that can realise Mind-essence through the right practice of dhyana, ought not to be sitting quietly with a blank mind nor wasting its resources on idle talk.) Do not talk all day about "the void, without practising it in the mind. One who does this may be likened to a self-styled king who is really a commoner. Prajna can never be attained in that way and those who act like that are not my disciples.

What is Prajna? It means, Transcendental Wisdom. If we steadily, at all times and in all places, keep our thoughts free from foolish desire and act wisely on all occasions, then we are practising the Paramita of Prajna. One foolish notion is enough to shut-off Prajna; one wise thought will bring it forth again. People in ignorance or under delusion do not see this; they talk about it with their tongue but in their mind they are ignorant of it. They are always saying that they practice Prajna, and they talk incessantly about "vacuity," but they have not realised the True Void. Prajna is Wisdom's Heart; it has neither form nor characteristic. If we interpret it in this way, then it is, indeed, the Wisdom of Prajna.

What is Paramita? It is a Sanskrit word (commonly translated, "ideal") that means, "to the opposite shore." Figuratively it means, "beyond existence and non-existence." By clinging to sense things, existence and non-existence are like the ups and downs of the billowy sea. Such a state, metaphorically is called, "this shore"; while beyond existence and non-existence there is a state characterised by non-attachment that has the undisturbed calmness of running water, that is called, "the opposite shore." This is why Prajna is called, Paramita.

Learned Audience: People under illusion recite the Maha Prajna-paramita with their tongue and, while they are reciting it, erroneous and evil thoughts arise; but if they put it into practice unremittingly they will come to realise its True Nature. To know this Dharma is to know the Law of Prajna; and to practice it is to practice Ideal Wisdom. He who does not practice it is an ordinary man; he who concentrates his mind on its practice, even if it be but for a moment only, he is the equal of Buddha. An ordinary man is Buddha! and defilement is Enlightenment (Bodhi). A passing foolish thought makes one an ordinary man, while an enlightened thought makes one a Buddha. A passing thought that clings to sense-objects is defilement; a second thought that frees one from attachment is Enlightenment.

Maha Prajna-paramita! The Great Transcendental-Wisdom Ideal, supreme, most exalted, foremost. It neither stays, nor goes, nor comes. By it Buddhas of the present, the past and future generations attain Buddhahood. We should use this Perfect Wisdom to break up the five bundles of aggregates that make up our personality, and thus get rid of the pollutions and contaminations. To follow such a practice ensures the attainment of Buddhahood. The three poisonous elements (greed, anger and infatuation) will then be turned into good conduct (*sila*) and self-realisation (*samadhi*) and wisdom (*Prajna*). When one is free from defilement, Wisdom reveals itself steadily and cannot be distinguished from Mind-essence. Those who understand this Dharma will be free from idle thoughts. To be free from discriminations, from clinging to desires, from illusions; to set free one's true nature; to use Prajna for contemplation; to take an attitude of neither indifference nor attachment towards all things—that is what is meant by realising one's true Essence of Mind and (in its perfection) is the attainment of Buddhahood.

Learned Audience: If you wish to penetrate the deepest mystery of the Dharma-world and experience the deepest realisation (*samadhi*) of Prajna, you should practice Prajna by reciting and studying the Diamond Sutra (*the Vajrakkhedika*) which will enable you to realise Essence of Mind. You should know that the merit for studying this Sutra is distinctly set forth in the text in laudatory terms; it is immeasurable and illimitable and cannot be enumerated in detail. This Sutra expounds the highest thought of Buddhism and our Lord Buddha delivered it specially for the very wise and quick-witted. The less wise and the slow-witted doubt its credibility. Why? For example: When it rains through the power of the celestial Naga on the plains of India, cities, towns and villages are drifted about as if they were only leaves of the date tree; but should it rain on the great ocean, the level of the seas of the whole world would not be affected by it. When the followers of the highest school of Mahayana study the Diamond Sutra, their minds become enlightened as they realise that Prajna is immanent in their own Mind-essence. Since they have their own access to highest wisdom through the constant practice of concentration and contemplation (dhyana and samadhi) they realise that they no longer need to rely on scriptural authority.

The Prajna immanent in the minds of every one may be likened to the rain, the moisture of which refreshes every living thing, trees and plants as well as sentient creatures. When rivers and streams reach the sea, the water carried by them merges into the one body, which is a good analogy. When rain falls in a deluge, plants which are not deep-rooted are washed away and eventually they perish. It is the same with the slow-witted when they hear about the teachings of the "Sudden School." The Prajna immanent in them is exactly the same as that in very wise men, but when the Dharma is made known to them they fail to enlighten themselves. Why is it? It is because their minds are thickly veiled by erroneous views and deeply rooted infections, just as the sun is often thickly veiled by clouds and unable to show its splendor until the wind blows the clouds away. Prajna does not vary with different persons; what makes the seeming difference is the question whether one's mind is enlightened or is beclouded. He who does not realise his own Mind-essence, and rests under the delusion that Buddhahood can be attained by outward religious rites, is rightly called the slow-witted. He who knows the teachings of the "Sudden School," and who attaches no importance to ritual, and whose mind always functions under right views so that he is absolutely free of defilement and contamination, such an one may be said to have realised his Mind-essence.

Learned Audience: The mind should be framed in such a way that it will be independent of external and internal things, at liberty to come and go, free from attachment, thoroughly enlightened, without the least obscuration. He whose mind is thus framed is able to measure up to the standard of the Prajna Sutras. The sutras and the scriptures of both the Mahayana and the Hinayana, as well as the twelve sections of the canonical writings, were provided to suit the different needs and temperaments of various people. It is upon the principle that Prajna is latent in every man that the doctrines expounded in these scriptures are established. If there were no human beings, there would be no teachings; hence we know that all teachings are made for man and that all the Sutras owe their existence to preachers. Some men are wise, the so called superior men, and some are ignorant, the so called inferior men; the wise preach to the ignorant when they are asked to do so. Through this the ignorant may attain sudden enlightenment and their minds will become illuminated thereby; then they are no longer different from wise men. Without enlightenment there would be a difference between a Buddha and any other living being; a gleam of enlightenment is enough to make a living being the equal of a Buddha. Since all truth (*Dharmas*) is immanent in our minds, there is no reason why we should not realise intuitively the real nature of Mind-essence (*tathata*). The Bodhisattva Sila Sutra says, "Our Essence of Mind is intrinsically pure; if we knew our mind perfectly and realised what our self-nature truly is, all of us would attain Buddhahood." The Vimalakirti Nirdesa Sutra says, "At once they become enlightened and regain their true mind."

When the Fifth Patriarch preached to me I became enlightened immediately after he had spoken and spontaneously I realised the real nature of Mind-essence (*tathata*). For this reason it is my particular object to propagate the teaching of the "Sudden" School so that learners may know enlightenment at once and realise their true nature by introspection of mind. Should they fail to enlighten themselves they ought to ask some very pious and learned Buddhist who understands the teachings of this highest school to show them the right way. The office of a pious and learned Buddhist who guides others to realise Essence of Mind, is an exalted position. Through his assistance one may be initiated into all meritorious Dharmas. The wisdom of Buddhas, past, present and future, as well as the teachings of the twelve sections of the canon are immanent in the mind, but in case we fail to enlighten ourselves, we have to seek the guidance of the pious and learned. On the other hand those who enlighten themselves need no extraneous help. It is wrong to insist upon the idea that we cannot obtain liberation without the assistance of the pious and learned. It is by our innate wisdom that we enlighten ourselves, and even the extraneous help and instruction of a pious and learned friend would be of no use so long as one is deluded by false doctrines and erroneous views. As we introspect our minds with Prajna, all erroneous views will disappear of themselves, and just as soon as we realise Essence of Mind we will immediately arrive at the Buddha stage.

When we use Prajna for introspection we are illuminated within and without and are in position to know our own nature. To realise our own nature is to obtain fundamental liberation. To obtain liberation is to attain the Samadhi of Prajna, which is intuitive insight. What is intuitive insight? Intuitive insight is to see and to realise all dharmas (things as well as truths) with a mind free from attachment. In action Prajna is everywhere present yet it "sticks" nowhere. What we have to do is to so purify the mind that the six aspects of consciousness (sight, sound, smell, taste, touch, mentation) in passing through their six sense-gates will neither be defiled by nor attached to their six sense-objects. When our mind works freely without any hindrance and is at liberty "to come" or "to go, "then we have attained the intuitive insight of Prajna, which is emancipation. To enable one to attain such a mental state of freedom is the function of intuitive insight. To refrain from thinking of anything, in the sense that all mental activity is suppressed, is to be Dharma-ridden; this is an extremely erroneous view. (Discriminative thought which leads to desire and attachment, or to aversion and defilement, is to be controlled in the interests of intuitive thought which leads to self-realisation and freedom.)

Those who understand the way of intuitive insight will know everything; they will have the experience that all the Buddhas have had, and they will attain Buddhahood. In the future, if an initiate of my school should make a vow in company with his fellow-disciples to devote his whole life without retrogression to the practice and commemoration of the teachings of this "Sudden" School, in the same spirit as if he were serving the Buddha, he would attain without failure the Path that leads to Bodhisattvahood and Buddhahood. He should transmit from heart the instructions handed down. from one Patriarch to another, and no attempt should be made to conceal the orthodox teaching.

Learned Audience: I have a Stanza for all of you to recite. Both laity and monks should put its teachings into practice, without which I t would be useless to remember the words alone. Listen to this stanza:—

A master of the Buddhist canon As well as the teachings of the Dhyana school Should teach nothing but the Dharma for realising Essence of Mind. We can hardly classify dharmas into "sudden" and "gradual," But some men will attain enlightenment quicker than others. For example: this system for realising Essence of Mind Is beyond the comprehension of the ignorant. We may explain it in ten thousand ways, p. 246 But all these explanations may be traced back to one principle, To illumine our gloomy mind, stained by defilement, We should constantly set up the Sun of Wisdom. Erroneous views keep us in defilement, But right views remove us far from it. But when we are in a position to discard both defilement and purity Then are we absolutely free. Bodhi is immanent in our Mind-essence; Any attempt to look for it elsewhere is foolish. Within our defiled minds, purity is to be found, And once our mind is set right, we are free from the bonds Of defilement, of evil karma, of expiation. If we are treading the Path of Enlightenment, We need not be worried by stumbling-blocks. If we keep an eye constantly on our own faults, We cannot go far astray from the right path. Every species of life has its own way of salvation; They will not be antagonistic one to another. If we leave our own path and seek for another way Of salvation, we shall never find it. Though we plod on till death overtake us We shall find only penitence at the end. If one wishes to find the true way, Right action will lead him to it directly. If one has not a mind to aim at Buddhahood, One will grope in the dark and never find it.

He who treads the Path in earnest Sees not the mistakes of the world. If we find fault with others, p. 247 We ourselves are also in the wrong; When other people are in the wrong we should ignore it; It is wrong for one to find fault with others. By getting rid of the habit of fault-finding, We get rid of one source of defilement. When neither hatred nor love disturb the mind, Serene and restful is our sleep. Those who intend to be teachers of others Should themselves be skillful in the various expedients that lead to enlightenment. When the disciple is free from all doubts Then it indicates that his Mind-essence is unclouded. This world is the Buddha-world Within which enlightenment may be sought. To seek enlightenment by separating from this worldIs as foolish as to search for a rabbit's horn. Right views are called "transcendental,"Erroneous views are called "worldly," But when all views, both right and erroneous, are discarded, Then the essence of Wisdom manifests itself. Kalpa after kalpa a man may be under illusion,_But once enlightened, it takes him but a moment to attain Buddhahood.

After hearing what the Patriarch had to say, Prefect Wai, the government officials, Taoists, monks and laymen, were all enlightened. They made obeisence in a body and exclaimed unanimously, "Well done! Well done! Who would have expected that a Buddha would be born in Kwongtung?"

Chapter III

Discourse on Dhyana and Samadhi

THE PATRIARCH, on another occasion, addressed the assembly as follows:—

Learned Audience: Samadhi and Prajna are fundamental. But you must not be under the wrong impression that they are independent of each other, for they are not two entities, they are inseparably united. Samadhi is the quintessence of Prajna, while Prajna is the activity of Samadhi. At the very moment that one attains Prajna, Samadhi is present; when one enters Samadhi, Prajna is present. If you understand this, you understand the—"Oneness—" of Samadhi and Prajna. A disciple should not think that there is a distinction between—"Samadhi begets Prajna,—" and—"Prajna begets Samadhi.—" To hold such an opinion would imply that these are two characteristics in the Dharma.

For one whose tongue is ready with good words but whose heart is impure, Samadhi and Prajna are useless because they are not in balance. On the other hand, when one is good in mind as well as in word, and when the outward appearance and inner feelings are in harmony with each other, then Samadhi and Prajna are in balance.

To an enlightened disciple (who has realised Prajna in Samadhi) discussion about it is unnecessary. To argue about Prajna or Samadhi as to which comes first, places one in the same position with those who are under delusion. Argument implies a desire to win, it strengthens egoism, it binds one to belief in the idea of—"a self, a being, a living being and a person.—" But we may liken Samadhi and Prajna to a glowing lamp and its light: with the glowing lamp there is light; without it there is darkness. Light is the quintessence of the glowing lamp, the glowing lamp is the expression of light. In name they are two things, but in reality they are one and the same. It is the same with Samadhi and Prajna.

The Patriarch continued: To practice samadhi is to make it a rule to have the mind in concentrated attention on all occasions (that is, not to let the mind wander from the thing in hand),—no matter what we are doing, walking, standing, sitting or reclining. The Vimalakirti Nirdesa Sutra says:" Straightforwardness is the holy place, the Pure Land.—" Do not let your mind be—"crooked—" and try to be straightforward with your lips only. People should practice straightforwardness but should not attach themselves to anything. People under delusion believe obstinately that there is a substance behind appearances and so they are stubborn in holding to their own way of interpreting the samadhi of specific mode, which they define as,—"sitting quietly and continuously without letting any idea arise in the mind.—" Such an interpretation would class us with inanimate objects; it is a stumbling-block to the right Path and the Path should be kept open. How can we block the Path? By attachment to any definite thought; if we free our minds from attachments, the Path will be clear, otherwise we are in bondage. If that practice of—"sitting quietly without letting any idea arise in the mind,—" is correct, why on one occasion was Saraputra reprimanded by Vimalakirti for sitting quietly in the forest? (That is, it is not thinking that blocks the Path, but attachment to definite thoughts.)

Some teachers of concentration instructed their disciples to keep a watch on their minds and secure tranquillity by the cessation of all thought, and henceforth their disciples gave up all effort to concentrate the mind and ignorant persons who did not understand the distinction became insane from trying to carry out the instruction literally. Such cases are not rare and it is a great mistake to teach the practice.

It has been the tradition of our school to make—"non-objectivity—" as our basis,—"idea-lessness—" as our object, and—"non-attachment—" as our fundamental principle.—"Non-objectivity—" means, not to be absorbed in objects when in contact with objects;—"idea-lessness—" means, not to be carried away by any particular idea in our exercise of the mental faculty; (—"non-attachment—" means, not to cherish any desire for or aversion to any particular thing or idea).—"Non-attachment—" is the characteristic of Mind-essence.

We should treat all things—good or bad, beautiful or ugly—as void (of any self-substance). Even in time of dispute and quarrel, we should treat intimates and enemies alike and never think of retaliation. In the thinking faculty, let the past be dead. If we allow our thoughts, past, present and future, to become linked up into a series, we put ourselves under restraint. On the other hand, if we never let our mind become attached at any time to any thing, we gain emancipation. For this reason we make—"non-attachment—" our fundamental principle.

To free ourselves from dependence upon externals is called,—"non-objectivity.—" In as far as we are in position to do this, the path of the Dharma is free. That is why we make—"non-objectivity—" our basis.

To keep our mind free from defilement under all circumstances is called—"idea-lessness.—" Our mind should always stand aloof and on no account should we allow circumstances to influence the functioning of the mind. It is a great mistake to suppress all thinking. Even if we succeed, and die immediately thereafter, still, there is reincarnation. Mark this, pilgrims of the Path! It is bad enough for a man to commit blunders by cherishing false ideas of the Dharma, how much worse to teach others. Being deluded, he is blind himself, and in addition he misrepresents and puts to shame the Buddhist scriptures. Therefore we make—"idea-lessness—" our object.

There is a type of man who is tinder delusion who boasts of his realisation of Mind-essence; but being influenced by circumstances ideas rise in his mind, followed by erroneous views, which in turn become the source of attachment and defilement. In Essence of Mind, intrinsically, there is nothing to be attained. To boast of attainment and to talk foolishly of merits and demerits is erroneous and defiling. For this reason we make—"idea-lessness—" the object of our school.

(If—"idea-lessness—" is not the cessation of all thought) what ideas should we get rid of, and on what ideas should we focus our mind? We should get rid of all—"pairs of opposites—" of all conceptions of goodness and badness (that is, of all discriminative thinking). We should focus our mind on the true nature of reality. (The word used is—"Tathata,—" which means,—"True Nature,—" or Mind-essence, or Prajna, or—"Oneness,—" or—"Suchness,—" or anything else that is ultimate.) Tathata (considered as the ultimate—"suchness—" of Mind-essence) is the quintessence of—"idea—";—"idea—" is the manifestation of Tathata. It is the function of Tathata to give rise to—"ideas.—" It is not the sense-organs that do so. Tathata (considered as the Intellective Principle) reproduces its own attribute, therefore, it can give rise to—"idea.—" Without Tathata, sense-organs and sense-objects would disappear immediately. Because it is an attribute of Tathata to give rise to ideas, our sense-organs, in spite of their functioning in seeing, hearing, touching, smelling and knowing, are not tainted and defiled under all circumstances. (It is the cherishing of—"attachments—" that defiles.) Our true-nature is—"self-manifesting—" all the time. (The Path to self-realisation of Mind-essence through Samadhi and Prajna is present to all, even though for some it may be blocked for a time by—"attachments.—") Therefore, the Sutra says:—"He who is an adept in appreciation of that which lies behind things and phenomena, is established upon the Ultimate Principle (Prajna).

The Patriarch one day preached to an assembly as follows:

In our system of Dhyana, we neither dwell upon our mind nor upon its purity; neither do we seek to suppress its activity. As to dwelling on the mind: the (functional) mind is primarily delusive and as we come to realise that it is only a phantasm we see that there is no reason for dwelling upon it. As to dwelling upon its purity: our nature is intrinsically pure, and just as far as we get rid of discriminative thinking, there will remain nothing but purity in our nature; it is these delusive ideas that obscure our realisation of True reality (Tathata). If we direct our mind to dwell upon purity, we are only creating another delusion: the delusion of purity. Since delusion has no abiding place, it is deluding to dwell upon it. Purity has neither shape nor form, but some people go so far as to invent the "Form of Purity" and then treat it as a problem for solution.' Holding such an opinion, these people become purity-ridden and their Essence of Mind is thereby obscured. Those who are training themselves for serenity of mind, in their contact with the many types of men, should not notice the faults of others. They should be indifferent as to whether others are good or bad, or whether they deserve merit or demerit. To assume a discriminatory attitude toward others is to invite perturbation of mind. An unenlightened man may seem outwardly unperturbed, but as soon as he opens his mouth and criticises others and talks about their merit or demerit, their ability or weakness, their goodness or badness, he shows that he has deviated from the right course. On the other hand, to dwell upon our own mind and its purity is also a stumbling-block in the true Path.

At another assembly the Patriarch spoke as follows: What is dhyana? It means, first, to gain full freedom of mind and to be entirely unperturbed under all outward circumstances, be they good or otherwise. What is the difference between Dhyana and Samadhi? Dhyana is the effort to be mentally free from any attachment to outer objects. Samadhi is the realisation of that freedom in inward peace. If we are attached to outer objects the inner mind will be perturbed. When we are free from attachment to all outer objects, the mind will be at peace. Our Essence of Mind is intrinsically pure; the reason we become perturbed is simply because we allow ourselves to be carried away by the circumstances we are under. He who is able to keep his mind serene, irrespective of circumstances, has attained true Samadhi.

To be free from attachment is Dhyana; to realise inner peace is Samadhi. When we are able to hold the mind concentrated, and to rest in inner peace, then we have attained both Dhyana and Samadhi. The Bodhisattva Sila Sutra says: "Our Essence of Mind is intrinsically pure." Learned Audience: let us each realise this for himself from one momentary sensation to another. Let us practice it by ourselves, let us train ourselves, and thus by our own effort attain Buddhahood.

Chapter IV

Discourse on Repentance

AT ONE TIME there was a large gathering of literary men and commoners gathered from Kwong-chow, Shiu-chow and other places, to listen to the Patriarch's words at his monastery of Tso-kai. The Patriarch ascended his platform and delivered the following address:—

Come, good people. In Buddhism we should start from our Essence of Mind. Let us purify our minds always and from one momentary sensation to another. Let us follow the Path by our own effort, recognise our own Essence-body, realise that our own mind is Buddha, and free ourselves by a voluntary observance of the disciplinary rules,—then this gathering will not be in vain. You have all come from distant places: and your gathering here shows the affinity that exists among us. Let us now sit down together in the Indian fashion for Dhyana, while I first lead you in the ritual of Repentance (*Ksamayati*).

When they were seated the Patriarch continued:—The first is the Sila Incense (Behavior), which symbolises that our minds are free from all taint of misdeeds, evil, jealousy, avarice, anger, spoilation and hatred. The second is Samadhi Incense, which symbolises that our mind is serene under all circumstances—favorable or unfavorable. The third is Prajna Incense, which means that our minds are free from all impediments; that we constantly seek to realise our Mind-essence with wisdom; that we refrain from all evil; that we do all kinds of good acts with no attachment to the fruit of such action; and that we are respectful toward our superiors, considerate of our inferiors, and sympathetic for the destitute and those in trouble. The fourth is the Incense of Liberation, which means that our minds are in such a perfectly free state that they cling to nothing and bother themselves neither with good nor evil. The fifth is the Incense of "Knowledge gained because of the attainment of Liberation." When our minds cling to neither good nor evil, we should take care not to let them go to the other extreme of vacuity and remain in a state of inertia. At this point we should study and seek to broaden our knowledge so that we can understand our own minds, thoroughly understand the principles of Buddhism, be considerate of others in our dealings with them, get rid of the idea of "self" and "existence," and realise that up to the time when we obtain enlightenment (*Bodhi*) our true nature (*Tathata*) is immutable.

Learned Audience:—This five-fold Incense perfumes us from within; we should not seek it without. Now I want to explain to you this Ritual of Repentance which is designed to expiate our sins whether committed in the present, the past or future lives; and whether physical, or by word, or by thought. (In Buddhist thought, sin is considered not in a legal sense as something to be punished, or forgiven, or atoned for by sacrifice, but in its cause-and-effect aspect of Karma and its maturing.)

Please follow me carefully and repeat together what I am going to say. May we, disciples (from such and such a village), be always free from the taint of ignorance and delusion. We repent of all our past, present and future sins and evil deeds committed under delusion or in ignorance. May their karma be expiated at once and may they never rise again.

May we, disciples (from such and such a village), be always free from taint of arrogance and dishonesty. We repent of all our past, present and future evil deeds done in an arrogant or dishonest spirit. May their karma be expiated at once and may they never rise again.

May we, disciples (from such and such a village), be always free from taint of envy and jealousy. We repent of all our past, present and future evil deeds done in an envious or jealous spirit. May their karma be expiated at once and may they never rise again.

As you will notice, there are two aspects to this repentance ritual: One refers to repentance for past sin; we ought to repent for all our past sins and evil deeds committed under delusion or ignorance, arrogance or dishonesty, jealousy or envy, so as to put an end to all of them. This is one aspect of repentance. The other aspect refers to future conduct. Having realised the evil nature of our transgression we make a vow that hereafter we will put an end to all evil deeds committed under delusion or ignorance, arrogance or dishonesty, envy or jealousy, and that we will never sin again. This is the second aspect of repentance. On account of ignorance and delusion, common people do not always appreciate that in repentance they must not only feel sorry for their past sins, but must also refrain from sinning in the future. Since they often take no heed as to their future conduct, they commit the same sins over again almost before the past ones are expiated. How can we call that repentance?

Learned Audience: Having repented of our sins, we should take the following all-embracing vows: Listen very carefully:—

Our Mind-essence is potential of an infinite number of sentient beings. We vow to bring them all unto deliverance.

We vow to get rid of the evil passions of our minds, inexhaustible though they seem.

We vow to learn the countless systems of Dharma in our Mind-essence.

We vow to attain the Supreme Buddhahood of our Mind-essence.

We have now vowed to deliver an infinite number of sentient beings; but what does that mean? It does not mean that I, Hui-neng is going to deliver them. And who are these sentient beings, potential within our minds? They are the delusive mind, the deceitful mind, the evil mind, and such like—all these are sentient beings. Each of them has to be delivered by oneself by means of his own Essence of Mind; only by his own deliverance, is it genuine.

Now, what does it mean, "delivering oneself by one's own Essence of Mind?' It means the deliverance of the ignorant, delusive, and the vexatious beings that spring up within our own mind, by means of Right Views. With the aid of Right Views and Prajna, the barriers thrown up by these delusive and ignorant beings may be broken down; so that each of us will be in a position to deliver himself by his own efforts. The false will be delivered by truthfulness; the delusive by enlightenment; the ignorant by wisdom; and the malevolent by benevolence; such is genuine deliverance.

As to the vow; "to get rid of the inexhaustible evil passions," that refers to the transcendence of our unreliable and illusive thinking faculty by the transcendental Wisdom (Prajna) of our Mind-essence. As to the vow: "to learn the countless systems of Dharma"; there will be no true knowledge until we have been brought face to face with our Essence of Mind, by our conforming to the orthodox Dharma on all occasions. As to the vow, "to attain Supreme Buddhahood"; I wish to point out that when we are able to control our mind to follow the true and orthodox Dharma on all occasions, and when Prajna always rises in our minds, so that we can hold aloof from both ignorance and enlightenment, and can do away with falsehood as well as truth, then we may consider ourselves as having realised our Buddha-nature, or, in other words, having attained Buddhahood.

Learned Audience: we should always bear in mind that we are following the Path for thereby strength is added to our vows. Now, since we have all taken the four-fold vows, I will teach you the Ritual of the threefold Guidance.

We take "Enlightenment" as our Guide, because it is the fruit of both merit (*Punya*) and Wisdom (*Prajna*).

We take "Orthodoxy" as our Guide, because it is the best way to get rid of desire.

We take "Purity" as our Guide, because it is the noblest quality of mankind.

Hereafter let Shakyamuni, the Enlightened One, be our guide and on no account should we listen to the suggestions of Mara, the evil one, of any heretic. We should testify to ourselves by constantly appealing to the "Three Gems" or our Essence of Mind, in which I advise you to take refuge. They are:

> *Buddha, which stands for Enlightenment;*
> *Dharma, which stands for Orthodoxy;*
> *Sangha, which stands for Purity.*

To take refuge in Enlightenment so that evil and delusive notions do not arise, so that desire decreases, discontent becomes unknown, and lust and greed no longer bind us—this is the fruitage of Punya and Prajna. To take refuge in Orthodoxy so that from momentary sensation to another we will be free from wrong views—this is the best means of getting rid of desires. To take refuge in Purity so that no matter under what circumstance we may be, we will not become contaminated by wearisome sense objects, by craving nor by desire—this is the noblest quality of mankind. To practise the "Three-fold Guidance" as thus outlined means to take refuge in one's Mind-essence. Ignorant people often take the "Three-fold Guidance" without understanding it. They say that they take refuge in Buddha: do they know where he is? If they cannot conceive Buddha, how can they take refuge in him? Would not such an assertion amount to self-deception? Each of you should examine this point for himself, so that his energy may not be misapplied through ignorance. The Sutra distinctly says that each should take refuge in the Buddha within himself. It does not refer to any other Buddhas, hence if we do not take refuge in the Buddha of our own Mind-essence, there is nowhere else for us to go. Having cleared this point, let each of us take refuge in the "Three jewels" of his own mind. Within, each should control his own mind; without, each should be respectful toward others—this is the way to take refuge within ourselves.

I have a stanza, the reciting and practising of which will at once dispel the delusions and expiate the sins accumulated during many kalpas. This is the stanza:—

People under delusion accumulate tainted merit but tread not the Path. They are under the illusion that to accumulate merit and to tread the Path are one and the same thing. Their merit for alms-giving and offerings may be infinite, But they fail to realise that the ultimate source of sin lies in the greed, hatred and infatuation within their own mind. They expect to expiate their sin by the accumulation of merit, Without knowing that the felicities to be gained thereby in future lives, Have nothing to do with expiation of sin. If we get rid of the sin within our own mind Then it is a case of true repentance. One who realises suddenly what constitutes true repentance in the Mahayana sense, And who ceases to do evil and practises righteousness, is free from sin.

Essence of Mind (Tathata) is the real Buddha, While heretical views and the three poisonous elements are Mara. Enlightened by Right Views, we call forth the Buddha within us. When our nature is dominated by the three poisonous elements, as the result of heretical views, We are said to be possessed by Mara; But when Right Views free our minds of these poison elements, Mara will, be transformed into a real Buddha. A follower of the Path who keeps constant watch on his Mind-essence Is in the same class with the many Buddhas. Our Patriarchs transmitted no other system but this of "Sudden Enlightenment." If you are seeking Dharmakaya, Search for it apart from the world of things and phenomena, Then your mind will be pure and free. Exert yourself in order to come face to face with Mind-essence and relax not; For death may come suddenly and put an end to your earthly existence.

Learned Audience:—All of you should recite this stanza and put it into practice. If you succeed in realising Essence of Mind, then you may think of yourselves as being in my presence though you may be a thousand miles away. But should you be unable to do so, though we were face to face with each other, we would really be thousands of miles apart. In that case what is the use of your taking the trouble to come here from such a long distance? Take good care of yourselves. I bid you good-bye.

Chapter V

Discourse on the Three-Bodies of Buddha

SOME TIME after the foregoing Discourse on Repentance had been delivered to "commoners" when the Patriarch had gathered his disciples together for instruction, a senior disciple, Fat-hoi, said to the Patriarch, "Sir, will you please leave to posterity certain instruction whereby people under delusion may realise their Buddha-nature?"

"Listen to me," replied the Patriarch. It is possible for those who are under delusion to realise their Buddha-nature, provided they acquaint themselves with the nature of ordinary sentient beings. Without such knowledge, to seek Buddhahood would be in vain, even if one spent aeons of time in doing so.

First, let me show you how to get acquainted with the nature of the sentient beings within your mind, whereby one can realise the Buddha-nature latent in everyone. Knowing Buddha means nothing else than knowing sentient beings. It is sentient beings who are blind to the fact that they are potentially Buddhas, whereas a Buddha sees no difference between himself and other beings. When sentient beings realise their Essence of Mind, they are Buddhas. If a Buddha is under delusion as to his Essence of Mind, he is then only an ordinary being. Seeing everything as equal in Essence of Mind makes ordinary beings Buddhas. Seeing inequalities in Essence of Mind transforms a Buddha into an ordinary being. When one's mind is crooked or depraved, then he is only an ordinary being with Buddha-nature latent within him. On the other hand, if one concentrates his mind on equality and straightforwardness, even for one moment only, then he is a Buddha.

Within our mind there is Buddha, and that Buddha within is the real Buddha. If Buddha is not to be found within our mind, then where shall we seek for the real Buddha? Doubt not that Buddha is within your own mind, apart from which nothing can exist. Since all things and phenomena are the product of mind, the Sutra says: "When mental activity rises, various things exist; when mental activity ceases, various things exist not."

Our physical body may be likened to an inn where we can remain only temporarily, we cannot make it a refuge. The Trikaya of Buddha is to be found within our Mind-essence which is the common possession of everybody. It is because the mind of an ordinary man labors under delusion that he does not know his own inner nature, the result is that he ignores the Trikaya that is within himself and seeks for it without. Please listen; I am going to show you that you can realise the Trikaya within yourself, which being a manifestation of Mind-essence cannot be found anywhere else.

Within our physical body we take refuge in the Pure Dharmakaya (Essence-body) of Buddha;_Within our physical body we take refuge in the Perfect Sambhoga-kaya (the Empirical, or Bliss-body) of Buddha;_Within our physical body we take refuge in the Myriad Nirmanakaya (Bodies of transformation, or of incarnations of Buddha.

What is the Pure Dharmakaya? Our Mind-essence is intrinsically pure, that is, all things are manifestations of mind. Good deeds and evil deeds are but the manifestation of good thoughts and evil thoughts respectively. Thus within Essence of Mind all things, like the azure of the sky and the radiance of the sun and moon which, when obscured by passing clouds, may appear as if their brightness had been dimmed, but as soon as the clouds are blown away, their brightness reappears and all objects are again fully illuminated. Foolish thoughts may be likened to the clouds, while sagacity and Wisdom are the moon and the Sun. When we become attached to discriminated objects, our Mind-essence becomes clouded by drifting thoughts which prevent sagacity and Wisdom from sending forth their light. We were fortunate that we found learned and pious teachers to make known the orthodox Dharma to us so that we may, by our own effort do away with ignorance and delusion, and by so doing we will become enlightened both within and without, and our true nature within our Essence of Mind will manifest itself. This is precisely what happens with those who come face to face with their Essence of Mind. This is what is called the Pure Dharmakaya of Buddha.

To take refuge in the true Buddha is to take refuge in our own Essence of Mind, He who takes refuge within himself must first get rid of the evil-mind and the jealous-mind, the flattering and crooked-mind, deceit, and falsehood, and fallacious views, egotism, snobbishness, contemptuousness, arrogance, and all other evils that may arise at any time, To take refuge within ourselves is to be always on the alert to prevent our own mistakes and to refrain from criticism of other's faults. He who is humble and patient on all occasions and is courteous to every one, has truly realised his Mind-essence, so truly in fact that his Path is free from further obstacles. This is the way to take refuge in (the Buddha of) oneself.

What is the Perfect Sambhogakaya? Let us take the illustration of a lamp. Since the light of a lamp can dissipate darkness that has been there for a thousand years, so a ray of Wisdom can do away with ignorance that has lasted for ages. We need not bother about the past, for the past is gone and is irrecoverable. What demands our attention is the present and future, so let our thoughts, from one momentary sensation to another, be clear and pure and let us see face to face our Mind-essence. Goodness and evil are opposite to each other, but in essence they cannot be dualistic. This non-dualistic nature is called "true nature," it can neither be contaminated by evil, nor affected by goodness. This is what is called the Sambhogakaya of Buddha. One single evil thought clouding our Essence of Mind will undo the good merit accumulated in aeons of time; while a good thought can expiate all our sins though they be as many as the sands of the river Ganges. To realise our Essence of Mind from one momentary sensation to another and without intermission until we attain Supreme Enlightenment (Bodhi) so that we are in a perpetual state of Right Mindfulness, is the Sambhogakaya.

Now, what is the Myriad Nirmanakaya? When we subject ourselves to the least differentiation or particularisation, transformation takes place: otherwise all things would be as void as space, as they inherently are. By letting our minds dwell on evil things, hell arises. By letting our minds dwell upon good acts, paradise is manifested. Dragons and snakes are the transformations of venomous hatred; while Bodhisattvas are compassionate thoughts made manifest. The various heavens are the projection of Prajna; while underworlds are the transformations of ignorance and infatuation. Un-numbered, indeed, are the transformations of Mind-essence. People under delusion are as if asleep; they do not understand; their minds naturally turn toward evil and, as a rule, they practice evil. But should they turn their minds from evil to righteousness, even for one moment, Prajna shines forth. This is what is called the Nirmanakaya of the Buddha of Mind-essence.

The Dharmakaya is intrinsically self-sufficient. To see our own Essence of Mind clearly and without interruption, is the Sambhogakaya of Buddha. To let our mind dwell on the Sambogahakaya, so that Prajna radiates forth in manifestation is Nirmanakaya. To attain enlightenment by one's own effort and to practise by one's self the goodness that is inherent in our Essence of Mind, is a genuine case of "taking refuge." Our physical body consisting of flesh and skin, etc., is nothing more than a tenement or an inn; it is no place of refuge. Let us realise the Trikaya of our own Mind-essence, then we shall know the Buddha of our own nature.

In closing let me leave with you a stanza, entitled: "The Real Buddha of Mind-essence." Accordingly as they heed it people of future generations who can understand its meaning will realise their Mind-essence and attain Buddhahood. This is the stanza:—

Those who understand the Mahayana teaching And are thus able to realise Mind-essence Should reverently and fervently seek for a realisation of Dharmakaya. The Dharmakaya, the Sambhogakaya, the Nirmanakaya— These three Bodies emanate from Oneness. He who is able to realise this fact intuitively_Has sown the seed and will reap the fruit of Enlightenment. It is from Nirmanakaya that our "pure nature" emerges; Within the former the latter is always to be found. Guided by its "pure nature" Nirmanakaya follows the right path,_And will some day culminate In a Body of Bliss, perfect and infinite._Pure Nature is hidden by our sensual instincts; By getting rid of sensuality, we realise Pure Dharmakaya. When our temperament is such that we are no longer the slave of the five sense-objects, And when we have realised Mind-essence, even for one moment, then Tathata is known to us. Those who are so fortunate as to be followers of the Sudden School Shall suddenly, in this life, see the Blessed One in their own Mind-essence. He who has not realised Essence of Mind and seeks for Buddha without, Is on a wrong path and is acting foolishly. He who seeks Buddha by practising certain doctrines Knows not the place where the real Buddha is to be found. He who is seeking to realise Buddha within his own mind, He only is sowing the seed of Buddhahood.

Chapter VI

Dialogues Suggested by Various Temperaments and Circumstances

UPON THE PATRIARCH'S RETURN to the village of Tso-hau in Shiu-chow from Wong-mui, where the Dharma had been transmitted to him, he was an unknown man. At that time, it was a Confucian scholar, named Liu Chi-luk, who first gave him a warm welcome and appreciation. It came about in this manner. Chi-luk had an aunt, named Wu Chun-chong who was a Buddhist nun, who was in the habit of reciting the Maha Parinirvana Sutra. One day the Patriarch heard her reciting it, and after listening for only a short time, grasped the profound meaning of the Sutra, and began to explain it to her, whereupon she brought the book and asked him the meaning of certain passages.

"I am not very well educated," he replied, "but if you wish to understand the purport of the book, I will do the best I can." "How can you understand the meaning of the text," she rejoined, "if you do not know the words?" To this he replied: "The profound teaching of the various Buddhas, has nothing to do with the written language."

This answer surprised her very much, and recognising that he was no ordinary man, she spoke of him freely to the pious elders of the village, saying: "He is a sage. We should get his permission to supply him with food and lodgings, and urge him to remain with us.

Whereupon a descendant of Marquis Wu of the Ai Dynasty, named, Tso Shuk-leung, came one afternoon with other villagers to offer homage to the Patriarch. At that time the historic Po-lam Monastery, which had been devastated by war at the end of the Chu Dynasty, was reduced to a heap of ruins. The villagers rebuilt it on the old site, and asked the Patriarch to make it his home. Afterwards it became a very famous temple.

THE MONK, FAT-HOI, a native of Hook-kong in Shui-chow, in his first interview with the Patriarch, asked the meaning of the well-known saying, "That which Mind is, Buddha is." The Patriarch replied, "Let not a vagrant thought rise up again, is 'Mind.' Let not a coming thought be repulsed, is 'Buddha.' To manifest all kind of phenomena, is 'Mind.' To be free from all form, is Buddha. If I were to give you a full explanation, it would take the full time of a kalpa. But listen to this stanza:

"Prajna is 'That which mind is'; Samadhi is 'what Buddha is.' In practising Prajna and Samadhi, let each keep pace with the other, Then our thoughts will be pure. This teaching can be understood Only through the 'habit of practice.' Samadhi functions, but inherently it is not. The orthodox teaching is, to practice Prajna as well as Samadhi."

After considering what the Patriarch had said, Fat-hoi was enlightened and he praised the Patriarch in the following stanza:

"That which mind is, Buddha is; how true it is, indeed! I put myself to shame by not understanding it. Now I understand the principle of Prajna and Samadhi, Both of which I shall practice to set myself free from all confining forms."

THE MONK FAT-TAT, a native of Hung-chow, who joined the order at the early age of seven, used to recite the Lotus of the Good Law Sutra. When he came to offer homage to the Patriarch, he failed in offering due respect to him, for which the Patriarch reproved him, saying, If you object to offer due respect, would it not be better to omit the salutation entirely? There must be something in your mind that makes you feel that way. Please tell me what you do in your daily religious exercise?

"I recite the Lotus of the Good Law (*Saddharma Pundarika*) Sutra," replied Fat-tat; I have read the whole text three thousand times."

"If you had fully understood the meaning of the Sutra," remarked the Patriarch, "You would not have assumed such a lofty bearing, even if you had read it ten thousand times. When you understand it, you will be following the same Path with me. But now, all that you have accomplished is to make yourself conceited. Moreover, you do not seem to realise that you are in the wrong. Listen to this stanza:

"Since the object of ceremony is to curb arrogance, Why did you fail to offer due respect? To take pride in oneself, is a source of sin, But to learn to treat any attainment as 'void,' is to attain incomparable merit."

The Patriarch then asked him for his name, and upon being told that his name was Fat-tat (which means "law-understanding"), he remarked, "Your name is Fat-tat, but you have not yet understood the Law." Then the Patriarch intending to conclude the interview, recited the following stanza:

"Your name is Fat-tat. Diligently and faithfully you recite the Sutra. Lip-repetition of the text ends with its pronunciation, But he whose mind is enlightened, by grasping its meaning, becomes a Bodhisattva. On account of conditions of affinity which may be traced to our past lives, Let me explain this to you. If you can only understand that Buddha speaks no words, Then the Lotus will blossom from your mouth. (Truth is inscrutable and ineffable; words fail, But the Lotus blossoms and radiates its perfume.)

Having heard this stanza, Fat-tat became ashamed and apologised to the Patriarch. He added, "Hereafter I will be humble and polite on all occasions. It is true: I do not quite understand the meaning of the Sutra as

I recite it, so I am often doubtful as to its proper interpretation. From your profound knowledge and high Wisdom, will you kindly give me a short explanation?"

The Patriarch replied: 'Tat-tat, the Good Law is quite clear; it is your mind that is not clear. The Sutra is free from doubtful passages; it is only your mind that makes them seem doubtful. Do you know the principal object of the Sutra?"

"How can I know, Sir," replied Fat-tat, "since I am so dull and stupid? All I know is to recite it word by word."

The Patriarch then said, "Will you please recite the Sutra? I am unable to read it myself. Then I will explain its meaning to you."

Fat-tat recited the Sutra loudly. When he came to the section entitled, "parables," the Patriarch stopped him, saying, "The theme of this Sutra is to set forth the aim and object of a Buddha's incarnation into this world. Though parables and illustrations are numerous in it, none of them go beyond this pivotal point. Now, what is that aim? and what is that object? The Sutra says, 'It is for a sole object, it is for a sole aim, but truly a lofty object and a lofty aim, that a Buddha appears in this world.' Now that sole object, that sole aim, that is so exalted, is the realisation of Buddha-knowledge.

"Common people attach themselves to external objects, thinking them to be real, and within, they fall into the wrong idea that external things come to an end. When they are able to free themselves from attachment to objects when in contact with objects, and to free themselves from the fallacious view that 'Emptiness' means annihilation, then they are free from illusions without and delusions within. He who understands this and whose mind is thus suddenly enlightened, is said to have opened his eyes to the sight of Buddha-Knowledge.

"The word, 'Buddha' is equivalent to 'Enlightenment' and is dealt with under four heads:--Opening the eyes for the sight of Enlightenment-knowledge; seeing the sight of Enlightenment-knowledge; understanding Enlightenment-knowledge; becoming firmly established in Enlightenment-knowledge. If we are able, upon being taught, to grasp and thoroughly understand the teaching of Enlightenment-knowledge, then our inherent quality of 'true-nature' will have an opportunity to manifest itself. You should not misinterpret the text and come to the conclusion that Buddha-knowledge is something special to Buddha and not common to us, just because you happen to find in the Sutra these passages: 'To open the eyes for the sight of Buddha-knowledge,' 'To see the sight of Buddha-knowledge, etc.' Such a misinterpretation would be slandering Buddha and blaspheming the Sutra. Since one is (potentially) a Buddha, he is already in possession of this Enlightenment-knowledge, and there is no occasion for him to open his eyes for it. You should therefore accept the interpretation that Buddha-knowledge is the Buddha-knowledge of your own mind and not that of any other Buddha.

"Being infatuated with sense-objects and thereby shutting themselves from their own light, all sentient beings, tormented by outer circumstances and inner vexations, act voluntarily as slaves to their own desires. Seeing this, our Lord Buddha took the trouble of rising from his Samadhi in order to exhort them by earnest preaching of various kinds to suppress their desires and to refrain from seeking happiness from without, so that they may enter into their rights of Buddhahood. For this reason the Sutra says, 'To open the eyes for Buddha-knowledge etc.' I advise people to thus constantly open their eyes for the Buddha-knowledge within their own minds. But in their perversity they commit sins under delusion and ignorance; they are kind in words but wicked in mind; they are greedy, malignant, jealous, crooked, flattering, egoistic, offensive to men and destructive to inanimate objects. Thus they open their eyes to 'common-people-knowledge' instead. Should they rectify their heart so that wisdom rises spontaneously, the mind is under introspection and the practice of doing good takes the place of evil. Thus they would initiate themselves into Buddha-knowledge.

"You should, therefore, from one momentary sensation to another, open your eyes, not for 'common-people-knowledge,' which is worldly, but for the Buddha-knowledge that is supra-mundane. On the other hand, if you stick to the arbitrary concept that mere recitation as a daily exercise is good enough, then you are infatuated, like the yak by its own tail."

Fat-tat then said: "If that is so, then we only have to know the meaning of the Sutra and there will be no further necessity for reciting it. Is that right, Sir?" The Patriarch replied, "There is nothing wrong with the Sutra that you need to refrain from reciting it. Whether sutra-reciting will enlighten you or not, or benefit you or not, all depends upon yourself. He who recites the Sutra with his tongue and puts its teachings into actual practice with his mind, masters the Sutra. Listen to this stanza:

"When our mind is under delusion, the Saddhama Pundarika Sutra is our master. When our mind is enlightened, we are the master of the Sutra. To recite the Sutra for a long time without knowing its principal object Indicates that one is a stranger to its meaning. To recite the Sutra without holding any arbitrary belief, is the correct way; To do otherwise is wrong. He whose mind is above 'affirmation' and 'negation' Rides permanently in the 'Buddha-vehicle.'"

Having heard this stanza, Fat-tat was enlightened and was unconsciously moved to tears. "it is quite true," he exclaimed, "heretofore I have been unable to master the Sutra, rather it has been my master."

Fat-tat then raised another difficulty. "The Sutra says, 'From various disciples up to Bodhisattva, though they were to speculate with their combined effort, they would be unable to comprehend Buddha-knowledge.' But you, Sir, give me to understand that if an ordinary man realises his own mind, he is said to have attained Buddha-knowledge. I am afraid, Sir, that with the exception of those gifted with superior mental dispositions, others may doubt your remark. Further, the Sutra mentions three kinds of carts: goat carts (the vehicle of disciples); deer carts (for Arahats); and bullock carts (for Bodhisattvas). How are these to be distinguished from the White Bullock carts of the Buddhas? Will you please tell me)"

The Patriarch replied: "The Sutra is quite plain on this point; it is you who fail to understand it. The reason why disciples, Arahats and Bodhisattvas fail to comprehend Buddha-knowledge is because they speculate about it (with their thinking mind which is limited and polluted); they may combine their efforts, but the more they speculate the farther they are from Truth. (Buddha-knowledge is to be realised within, not thought about as though it was something external.) It was not to Buddhas but to ordinary men that Buddha Gautama preached this Sutra. You do not seem to appreciate that since we are already riding in the White Bullock cart of the Buddhas, that there is no necessity for us to look for other vehicles. Moreover, the Sutra plainly teaches that there is only the one Buddha vehicle; that there are no others, no second, no third. It is because there is only one vehicle that Buddha had to preach to us with innumerable skillful means such as various reasons and argument, various parables and illustrations, etc. Do you not understand that the other three vehicles are makeshifts, useful for the past only; while the sole vehicle, the Buddha vehicle, is for the present because it is ultimate?

"The Sutra teaches to dispense with the makeshifts and depend on the ultimate. Having resorted to the ultimate, you will find that even the very name 'ultimate' disappears. You should appreciate that you are the sole owner of these treasures and that they are entirely subject to your disposal. (This is in allusion to another Parable, the Buddhist Prodigal Son, in the Sutra.) But moreover, it is not until you are able to free yourself from the arbitrary conceptions that there are any treasures belonging to the Father or to the son, or subject to so and so's disposal, that you really know the right way to recite the Sutra. When you so understand it, the Sutra will be in your hand from eternity to eternity, and from morning to midnight you will be reciting the Sutra all the time."

Being thus awakened, Fat-tat praised the Patriarch in a transport of joy with the following stanza:--

"The delusion that I had attained great merit by reciting the Sutra three thousand times Is all dispelled by a single utterance of the Master of Tso-kai. He who has not yet under-stood the object of the Buddha's incarnation Is unable to suppress the wild passions accumulated in many lives. The three vehicles are makeshifts only; And the three stages in which the scholars expound the Dharma are ingeniously spoken, indeed; But how few appreciate that it is within the burning house itself That the Truth of Dharma is to be found."

The Patriarch then told him that before he had rebuked him for being a "sutra-reciting monk," but that hereafter he would praise him for the same reason. After that interview, Fat-tat was able to grasp the profound meaning of Buddhism, and yet he continued to recite the Sutra as before.

THE MONK, SHI-TONG, a native of Shau-chow of An-fung, had read over the Lankavatara Sutra nearly a thousand times, but could not understand the meaning of the Trikaya nor the four Prajnas. One day he called upon the Patriarch for an explanation of them.

"As to the 'Three Bodies,'" explained the Patriarch, "The Pure Dharmakaya is your nature, The Perfect Sambhogakaya is your wisdom; and the Myriad Nirmanakayas are your actions. If you deal with these three bodies apart from your Mind-essence, they would be bodies without wisdom. If you realise that these three: self-nature, self-wisdom and self-action, have no substance of their own (being only manifestations of Mind-essence) then you have attained the enlightenment of the four Prajnas. Listen to this stanza:—

"The Three-bodies are inherent in our Essence of Mind, By the radiation of which the four Prajnas are manifested. Thus, without closing your eyes and your ears to shut out the external world, You may reach Buddhahood directly. Now that I have made this plain to you, If you believe it implicitly, you will be forever free from delusion. Follow not those who seek for 'enlightenment' from without: Such people talk about Bodhi all the time, but do it vainly."

For the second time, Chi-tong asked, "May I know something about the four Prajnas?" "If you understand the Three-Bodies," replied the Patriarch, "you should know the four Prajnas as well; your question is quite unnecessary. If you deal with the four Prajnas apart from the Three-Bodies, there would be Prajnas without bodies; in such a case, they would not be Prajnas. (Prajna is the Ultimate Principle of the Three-Bodies, which is Ultimate Reality.) The Patriarch then uttered this stanza:—

"Mirror-like Wisdom is pure by nature; Wisdom that comprehends all things equally, frees the mind from all impediments; All-discerning Wisdom sees things intuitively; All-performing Wisdom, like Mirror-Wisdom, is free from prejudice. Perception-consciousness of the five-sense-vijnanas, And the Universal Consciousness of the Alaya-vijnana, Are not 'transmuted' to Prajna, until the Buddha-stage; While the intellective-consciousness of the Manas, And the discriminative-consciousness of the Manovijnana, Are 'transmitted' in the Bodhisattva-stage. When you are able to free yourself entirely from attachments to sense-objects as these 'transmutations' take place, Then you will forever abide in the never-ceasing Naga Samadhi."

Suddenly Chi-tong realised the Prajna of his Mind-essence and submitted the following stanza to the Patriarch:—

"Intrinsically, the Three-Bodies are within our Essence of Mind. When our mind is enlightened, the four Prajnas will appear. When 'Bodies' and Prajna appear as one identity, Then are we able to respond to the appeal of all beings. no matter what form they take. To make an effort to find the Trikaya and the four Prajnas is to take an entirely wrong course; To try to 'discriminate' and 'grasp' them is to misunderstand their intrinsic nature. Through you, Sir, I am now able to realise the profundity of their meaning; Henceforth, I may discard for ever their false and arbitrary names."

THE MONK, CHI-SHEUNG, a native of Kwai-kai of Shun-chow, joined the order in his childhood and was very zealous in his efforts to realise Mind-essence. One day he came to pay homage to the Patriarch and was asked by the latter whence and for what he came. Chi-sheung replied:—

"I have recently been at the White Cliff Monastery in Hung-chow, to study with the Master Ta-tung who was good enough to teach me how to realise Mind-essence and thereby to gain Buddhahood, but as I still have some doubts, I have travelled far to come here to pay my respects to you. Will you kindly clear away my doubts, Sir?"

The Patriarch asked, "What instruction did he give you? Will you please repeat it."

Chi-sheung replied: "After staying there three months without receiving any instruction, and being zealous for the Dharma, I went alone one night to his chamber and asked him, what my essence of mind was. He asked me, 'Do you see the illimitable void?' 'Yes, I do,' I replied. Then he asked me whether the void had any particular form, and on replying that the void must be formless and therefore can not have any particular form, he said: 'Your Essence of Mind is exactly like the void. To realise that there is nothing to be seen, is Right View. To realise that nothing is knowable, is True Knowledge. To realise that it is neither green nor yellow, neither long nor short; that it is pure by nature; that its quintessence is perfect and clear; is to realise Essence of Mind and thereby to attain Buddhahood. This is also called, Buddha-knowledge.' As I do not quite understand this teaching, will you please enlighten me, Sir?"

"His teaching indicates," said the Patriarch, "that he still retains the arbitrary concepts of 'Views' and 'Knowledge'; that explains why he failed to make it clear to you. Listen to this stanza:—

"To realise that nothing can be seen, but to retain the concept of 'invisibility' Is somewhat like passing clouds obscuring the face of the sun. To realise that nothing is knowable, but to retain the concept of 'unknowability' May be likened to the clear sky disfigured by a flash of lightning. To let these arbitrary concepts rise spontaneously in the mind Indicates that you have not yet realised Essence of Mind, And that you have not yet found the skillful means to realise it. If you realise for one moment that these arbitrary concepts are wrong, Then your own spiritual light will shine forth unhindered."

Having heard this, Chi-sheung at once felt that his mind was enlightened. Thereupon, he submitted to the Patriarch, the following stanza:—

"To allow the concepts of 'invisibility' and 'unknowability' to rise spontaneously in the mind Is to seek Bodhi without freeing oneself from the arbitrary concepts of phenomena. He who is puffed-up by the slightest impression, 'I am now enlightened' Is no farther advanced than one under delusion. Had I not put myself at the feet of Your Eminence, I would have remained bewildered, ignorant of the right way to go."

One day Chi-sheung asked the Patriarch, "Buddha preached the doctrine of 'Three Vehicles' and also that of the 'Supreme Vehicle.' I do not understand them; will you please explain them to me?"

The Patriarch replied, "(In trying to understand these) you should introspect your own mind and ignore outward things and phenomena. The distinction of these four vehicles does not exist in the Dharma itself, but in the differentiations of people's minds. To see and to hear and to recite the Sutras, is the Small Vehicle. To know the Dharma and to understand its meaning is the Middle Vehicle. To put the Dharma into actual practice, is the Great Vehicle. To understand all Dharmas (intuitively), to become part of them, to be free from all attachments, to be independent of things and phenomena; to be in possession of nothing, that is the Supreme Vehicle.

"Essence of Mind is always a state of tranquillity. Since the word 'vehicle,' means, 'motion,' discussion is out of place. All depends on intuitive self-practice. Do not ask any more questions."

Chi-sheung made obeisance and thanked the Patriarch and, thereafter served as one of the Patriarch's personal attendants until his death.

THE MONK, CHI-WANG, a follower of the Dhyana school, had a consultation with the Fifth Patriarch and afterward considered himself to have attained Samadhi. For twenty years he confined himself to a small temple and all the time kept the Dhyana posture. Un-chak, a disciple of the Sixth Patriarch, on a pilgrimage to the northern bank of the Hoang-ho, heard about him and called at his temple.

"What are you doing here?" enquired Un-chak.

"I am abiding in Samadhi," replied Chi-wang.

"Abiding in Samadhi, did you say?" Observed Un-chak. "I wish to enquire whether you are doing it consciously or unconsciously? If you are doing it unconsciously, it would mean that it is possible for all inanimate objects, such as earthern ware, stones, trees and weeds, to attain Samadhi. On the other hand, if you do it consciously, then any animate object or sentient being might abide in Samadhi, also."

Chi-wang then said, "When I am in Samadhi, I know neither consciousness nor unconsciousness."

"In that case," observed Un-chak, "it is a perpetual quietude, in which there is neither abiding nor leaving. A state of samadhi in which you can abide or come out of at will, can not be a perfect Samadhi."

Chi-wang was nonplused. After a long time, he asked, "May I know who is your teacher?"

"My teacher is the Sixth Patriarch, of Tso-kai," replied Un-chak.

"How does he define Dhyana and Samadhi?" enquired Chi-wang.

"According to his teaching," replied Un-chak, "the Dharmakaya is perfect and serene and unchanging; its quintessence and its function are in a state of 'Suchness.' The five aggregates are intrinsically void and the six sense-objects are non-existent. There is neither abiding nor leaving in Samadhi;

there is neither quietude nor perturbation. The nature of Dhyana is non-abiding, so we should seek to transcend the state of 'abiding in the calmness of Dhyana.' The nature of Dhyana is uncreative, so we should transcend the notion of 'creating a state of Dhyana.' Essence of Mind is like space without the limitations of space."

After this interview, Chi-wang went to Tso-kai to interview the Sixth Patriarch. Upon being asked whence he came, Chi-wang told the Patriarch the details of his conversation with Un-chak.

The Patriarch said, "What Un-chak said is quite right. Let your mind be in a state like the illimitable void, but do not think of it as 'vacuity.' Let the mind function freely, but whether it is in activity or at rest, let it abide nowhere. Forget all discriminations: see no distinction between a sage and an ordinary man; ignore the distinction between subject and object; let Essence of Mind and all phenomena and objects be alike in a state of 'Suchness.' Then you will truly be in Samadhi all the time."

Chi-wang was thereby fully enlightened. What he had considered for the past twenty years as an attainment, now all vanished. He remained with the Patriarch for a time and then returned to Ho-Pei where he taught many people, monks as well as laymen.

THE MONK, CHI-TAO, a native of Nam-hoi of Kwongtung, came to the Patriarch for instruction, saying, "Since I joined the order, I have read the Maha Parinirvana Sutra for more than ten years, but I have not yet grasped its teaching. Will you please teach me."

"What part of it do you not understand?" enquired the Patriarch.

"It is this part, Sir: 'All things are impermanent and so they belong to the Dharma of Becoming and Cessation. When both Becoming and Cessation cease to operate, Cessation of Change with its bliss of Perfect Rest (Nirvana) arises.'"

"What obscurity is there in that? "enquired the Patriarch.

Chi-tao replied, "All beings have two bodies: the physical body and an essence body. The former is impermanent--it exists and it deceases. The latter is permanent, but it knows not and feels not. Now the Sutra says, 'When both Becoming and Cessation cease to operate, the bliss of Perfect Rest and Cessation of Change arises.' I can not understand which body ceases to exist, and which body enjoys the bliss. It cannot be the physical body that enjoys, because when it dies, the material elements disintegrate and disintegration is suffering, the very opposite of bliss. If it is the essence body that ceases to exist, it would be in the same 'unfeeling' state as inanimate objects, such as the grass, trees and stones. Who, then, will be the enjoyer?

"Moreover, essence-nature is the quintessence of 'Becoming and Cessation' whose manifestation is the union of the five 'aggregates' (body, sensation, perception, consciousness and intellection). That is to say, from one essence, five functions arise. This process of Becoming and Cessation is everlasting.

When function and operation 'arise' from the quintessence, it becomes; when operation and function are 'absorbed' back into the quintessence, it ceases to exist. If reincarnation is admitted, there will be no Cessation of Changes, as in the case of sentient beings. If reincarnation is out of the question, then things will remain forever in a state of lifeless quintessence, like the case of inanimate objects. When this is the case, under the limitations and restrictions of Nirvana, even existence would be impossible to all things, much less enjoyment."

"You are a Bhikkhu," said the Patriarch, "how can you adopt the fallacious views of Eternalism and Annihilationism that are held by heretics, and venture to criticise the teaching of the Supreme Vehicle? Your argument implies that apart from the physical body, there is an essence body; and that Perfect Rest and Cessation of Change may be sought apart from 'Becoming and Cessation.' Further, from the statement, 'Nirvana is everlasting rest,' you infer that there must be somebody to play the part of enjoyer.

"It is exactly these fallacious views that makes people crave for sentiate existence and worldly pleasure. These people are the victims of ignorance; they identify the union of the five aggregates as the 'self' and regard all other things as 'not-self'; they crave for individual existence and have an aversion to death; they are drifting about from one momentary sensation to another in the whirlpool of life and death without realising the emptiness of mundane existence which is only a dream and an illusion; they commit themselves to unnecessary suffering by binding themselves to rebirth; they mistake the state of everlasting joy of Nirvana to be a mode of suffering; they are always seeking after sensual pleasures. It was for these people, victims of ignorance, that the compassionate Buddha preached the real bliss of Nirvana.

"Never for a moment was Nirvana either the phenomena of Becoming and Cessation, or the ceasing of Becoming and Cessation. It is the perfect manifestation of Rest and Cessation of Change, and at the 'time' of manifestation, there is no such thing as manifestation. It is called 'everlasting' joy because it has neither enjoyer nor non-enjoyer.

"There is no such thing as 'one quintessence and five manifestations.' You are slandering Buddha and blaspheming the Dharma, when you go so far as to state that under the limitation and restriction of Nirvana, living is impossible to all beings. Listen to this stanza:--

"The Supreme Maha Parinirvana Is perfect, permanent, calm. radiantly illuminative. Common and ignorant people miscall it death. While heretics arbitrarily declare it to be annihilation. Those who belong to the Small Vehicle and to the Middle Vehicle Regard Nirvana as 'non-action.' All these are merely intellectual speculations, And they form the basis of the sixty-two fallacious views. Since they are merely names, invented for the occasion, They have nothing to do with Absolute Truth. Only those of super-eminent mind Can understand thoroughly what Nirvana is, And take an attitude toward it of neither attachment nor indifference. They

know that the five aggregates, And the so-called 'self' arising from the aggregates, Together with all external forms and objects, And the various phenomena of words and voice, Are all equally unreal, like a dream or an illusion. They make no discrimination between a sage and an ordinary man, Nor do they have any arbitrary Concept of Nirvana. They are above 'affirmation' and 'negation'; They break the barriers between the past, the present. and the future. Thy use their sense organs when occasion requires, But the concept of 'using' does not arise. They may particularise on all sorts of things._But the concept of 'particularisation' arises not. Even during the cataclysmic fire at the end of a kalpa. When ocean beds are burnt dry; Or during the blowing of catastropic winds, when mountains topple; The everlasting bliss of Perfect Rest and Cessation of Change that is Nirvana Remains the same and changes not."

The Patriarch then said to Chi-tao, "I am trying to describe to you something that intrinsically is ineffable, in order to help you to get rid of fallacious views. If you do not interpret my words too literally you may perhaps know a wee bit of Nirvana."

Chi-tao became highly enlightened and, in a rapturous mood he made obeisance and departed.

Chapter VII

Sudden Enlightenment and Gradual Attainment

CONTEMPORANEOUS WITH the Patriarch when he was living at Po-lam Monastery was Grand Master Shin-shau who was preaching in Yuk-chuen Monastery of King-nam. At that time the two schools of Hui-neng in the South and of Shin-shau in the North were both flourishing. As the two schools were distinguished from each other by the names, Sudden, and Gradual, some Buddhist scholars were troubled as to which school to follow.

One day the Patriarch addressed his assembly as follows:—

"So far as the Dharma is concerned, there can be only one school. If a distinction is made, it exists in the fact that the founder of one school was a Northern man, and the founder of the other was a Southern man. While there is only one system of Dharma, some disciples realise it quicker than others but the reason why the names, 'Sudden' and 'Gradual,' are given is because some disciples are superior to others in their mental dispositions. So far as the Dharma is concerned, the distinction of Sudden and Gradual does not exist."

(Between the two leaders there was mutual respect but) the followers of Shin-shau often criticised the Patriarch. They discredited him by saying that he was illiterate and could not distinguish himself in any respect. Shin-shau, on the other hand, admitted that he was inferior to the Patriarch in one respect, namely, that Hui-neng thoroughly understood the teachings of the Mahayana, even if he had attained that wisdom without the aid of a teacher. "Moreover," he added, "my Master, the Fifth Patriarch, would not have personally transmitted the robe and bowl to him without good cause: I regret that, owing to the patronage of the Court, which I by no means deserve, I am unable to travel far to receive instruction from him personally. You should go to Tso-kai to consult him. Do not tarry."

One day, Shin-shau said to his disciple, Chi-shing, "You are clever and witty; I wish you would go to Tso-kai and attend the lectures there. Try your best to keep in mind what you hear, so that on your return you may repeat it to me."

Acting on his teacher's instruction, Chi-shing arrived at Tso-kai. Without saying anything about where he came from, he joined the company attending the Patriarch's lectures. When the Patriarch came to address the assembly, he said, "Some one has come here secretly to learn my teaching and later to plagiarise it." Chi-shing at once came forward, made obeisance, and told the Patriarch what his mission was.

"You come from Yuk-chuen Monastery, do you?" said the Patriarch. "Then you must be a spy."

"No, I am not," replied Chi-shing. "Why not?" asked the Patriarch. "If I had not told you, I would have been a spy," said Chi-shing. "Since I have told you who I am, I am no spy."

"Tell me, how does your teacher instruct his disciples?" asked the Patriarch.

"He often tells them to concentrate their minds in a meditation on 'purity'; to keep up the dhyana position constantly, and not to lie down."

Said the Patriarch, "To concentrate the mind on a meditation on 'purity' is an infirmity and is not Dhyana. To restrict oneself to the cross-legged position all the time is logically unprofitable. Listen to this stanza:—

"A living man sits and does not lie down; But a dead man lies down and does not sit. On this physical body of ours, why should we impose the task of sitting crosslegged?"

Making obeisance a second time, Chi-shing remarked, "Though I have studied Buddhism for nine years under Grand Master Shin-shau, my mind was not awakened for enlightenment, but as soon as you speak to me, my mind is enlightened. As the question of continuous re-birth is an important one, I wish you would take pity on me and give me instruction as to that question."

The Patriarch said, "I understand that your Master gives his disciples instruction as to 'disciplinary rules' (sila), meditation (dhyana), and Wisdom (*Prajna*). Will you please, tell me how he defines these terms?"

"According to his teaching," replied Chi-shing, "to refrain from all evil action, is Sila; to practise whatever is good, is Prajna; and to purify one's mind, is Dhyana. This is the way he teaches us. May I ask what your system is?"

The Patriarch replied, "If I should tell you that I had a system of Dhyana to transmit to others, I would be deceiving you. What I try to do to my disciples, is to liberate them from their own bondage, by such device as each case requires. To use a name, which after all is nothing but a makeshift, it may be called 'Samadhi.' The way your Master teaches Sila, Dhyana, Prajna, is wonderful; but my way is different."

"How can it be different, Sir, when there is only one form of Sila, Dhyana and Prajna?"

"The teaching of your Master," replied the Patriarch, "is for the guidance of the general followers of the Mahayana; my teaching is for the more advanced followers. It is because some realise the Dharma quicker and deeper than others, that there is a difference of interpretation. Listen while I explain and see if you think my instruction is the same as his. In expounding the Dharma, I do not deviate from the authority of my intuitive mind. To do otherwise would indicate that the expositor's Mind-essence was obscured, and that he was competent to teach only the phenomenal side of the Dharma (but not its essence). The true teaching of Sila, Dhyana and Prajna, should be based on the principle that the function of all things derives its virtue from its essence. Listen to this stanza:—

"To free the mind from all improprieties is the Sila of Mind-essence; To free the mind from all perturbations is the Dhyana of Mind-essence. That which neither increases nor decreases is the 'diamond' of Mind-essence.' 'Going' and 'coming' are only phases of Samadhi."

Having heard this instruction, Chi-shing felt humiliated and thanked the Patriarch for the instruction.

The Patriarch continued: "The teaching of your Master on Sila, Dhyana and Prajna, is fitted for minds of wise men, it is true, but my teaching is intended for minds of a more advanced type. He who has realised Mind-essence, himself, may dispense with such doctrines as Bodhi, Nirvana, and Knowledge of Emancipation. It is only those who do not possess a single system of Dhyana, who can formulate all systems of Dhyana; these who understand what this means, may rightly use such terms as Buddhakaya, Bodhi, Nirvana, Knowledge of Emancipation. To those who have realised Mind-essence, it makes no difference whether they formulate all systems of Dhyana, or dispense with all of them. (Because of this non-attachment) they are at liberty to come or to go; they are free from all obstacles and impediments. As circumstances arise, they take appropriate action; they give suitable answers according to the varying temperament of their questioner. They see with a comprehensive glance that all 'Bodies of Transformation' are inseparable from Essence of Mind. They attain liberation, psychic powers, and Samadhi, which enables them to perform the arduous task of universal salvation as easily as if they were only playing. Such are the men who have realised Mind-essence.

"By what principle are we guided in dispensing with all systems of Dhyana?" was Chi-shing's next question.

The Patriarch replied:—"When our Mind-essence is free from improprieties, infatuations and perturbations; when we look inward from each momentary sensation to another, with Prajna; and when we no longer cherish attachment to objects, or to words, or to ideas; then are we forever emancipated. Why should we formulate any system of Dhyana when our goal may be reached no matter whether we turn to the right or to the left? Since it is by our own effort that we realise Mind-essence, and since the realisation and practise of Dhyana are both spontaneous and instantaneous, the formulation of any system of Dhyana is unnecessary. All Dharmas are intrinsically Nirvanic, how can there be gradation in them?"

Chi-shing made obeisance and volunteered to be an attendant of the Patriarch, in which capacity he served faithfully.

SINCE THE Two Dhyana Schools, that of Hui-neng in the South and Shin-shau in the North, were flourishing at the same time, in spite of the tolerant spirit shown by both Masters who hardly knew what egotism was, there naturally developed a strong sectarian feeling among the disciples. Calling their own Master, Shin-shau, the Sixth Patriarch on no better authority than their own wishes, the followers of the Northern School were jealous of the rightful owner of that title whose claim was supported by the possession of the insignia, the robe etc., and was generally acknowledged. (In order to get rid of the rightful Patriarch) they sent a lay member of the order whose secular name was Chang Hang-chong, a native of Kiang-si, and who as a young man had been fond of adventure, to get rid of him.

With his psychic power of mind-reading, the Patriarch was able to know of the plot. One evening Chang entered the Patriarch's room intending to carry out his instructions. The Patriarch, after placing ten taels near his side, bent his neck forward and waited the blow. Chang made three attempts, but strange to say no wound was made. Then the Patriarch spoke to him, saying,

"A straight sword is not crooked;
A crooked sword is not straight.
I owe you money only, but life I do not owe you."

Chang -was taken by surprise and, remorseful and penitent, he asked for mercy and volunteered to join the order at once, but the Patriarch handed him the money and said; "If my followers should learn of it, they would harm you; you must not remain here. Some other time come to see me in disguise and I will take good care of you." As directed, Chang ran away that night and subsequently joined the order under another Master. Upon being fully ordained, he proved himself to be a very diligent monk.

One day recollecting what the Patriarch had said, he made the long journey to see him and to pay him homage. "Why have you waited so long?" said the Patriarch, "I have been expecting you all the time."

Said Chang, "Since that night you so graciously pardoned my crime, I have become a monk and have studied Buddhism diligently. I can only show my gratitude adequately by spreading the Dharma for the deliverance of all sentient beings." Then he asked a question as to the meaning of "eternal and non-eternal," which the Patriarch answered and then said, "You have now thoroughly realised Mind-essence; hereafter you may call yourself, Chi-chai."

Chi-chai made obeisance and departed.

Chapter VIII

Royal Patronage

AN EDICT DATED the 15th day of the First Moon of the 1st year of Shin Lung, issued by the Empress Dowager Chek Tin and the Emperor Chung Chung, read as follows:—

"Since we have invited Grand Masters Wei-on and Shin-shau to stay in the Palace and receive our offerings, we have continued to study under them as far as we could find time after attending to our imperial duties. Out of sheer modesty, these two Masters recommended that we should seek the advice of Dhyana Master Hui-neng of the South, who had inherited the secret Dharma and the robe of the Fifth Patriarch as well as the 'Heart Seal' of the Lord Buddha.

"We hereby send Eunuch, Sit Kan, as the courier of this Edict to invite His Eminence to come, and we trust His Eminence will graciously favor us with an early visit, etc., etc."

On the ground of illness, the Patriarch sent a reply declining the royal invitation and craved permission to be allowed to spend his remaining years in the "forest." (In due time Sit Kan, the imperial envoy, arrived at Tso-kai and interviewed the Patriarch as follows):

"In the capitol, Dhyana experts unanimously advise people to meditate in the 'crosslegged' position to attain Samadhi; they say that this is the only way to realise the 'Norm' and that it is impossible for any one to obtain liberation without going through this meditation exercise. May I know your way of teaching, Sir?"

"The Norm is to be realised by the mind," replied the Patriarch, "it does not depend upon the crosslegged position. The Vajrakkhedika Sutra says that it is wrong 'for any one to assert that Tathagata comes or goes, sits or reclines.' Why? Because Tathagata's Dhyana of Purity implies neither coming from anywhere nor going to anywhere, neither becoming nor annihilation. All Dharmas are calm and void, such is Tathagata's Seat of Purity. Strictly speaking, there is no such thing as 'attainment'; why should we bother ourselves about the crosslegged position?"

"Upon my return," said Sit Kan, "Their Majesties will ask me to make a report. Sir, will you kindly give me some hints as to your essential teachings, so that I may make them known, not only to Their Majesties, but also to all Buddhist scholars at the Capital. As the flame of one lamp may kindle hundreds of thousands of others, the ignorant will be enlightened and light will produce light without end."

"The Norm implies neither light nor darkness," replied the Patriarch. "Light and darkness signify the idea of alternation. (It is not correct to say) 'light will produce light without end'; since light and darkness are a pair of opposites, there must be an end as well as a beginning. The Vimalakirti Nirdesa Sutra says, 'The Norm has no analogy; it is not a relative term.'"

"Light signifies wisdom, and darkness signifies defilement. If a pilgrim of the Path does not get rid of defilement by wisdom, how is he going to free himself from the 'wheel of birth and death,' which is beginningless?"

The Patriarch continued, "Defilement (*klesa*) is wisdom (*bodhi*); The two are the same and are not different from each other. To break up klasa by Bodhi is only a teaching of the followers of the 'Small' and 'Middle' vehicles. To those of keen intellect and superior mental attainment, such teaching is disapproved."

"What, then, is the teaching of the Mahayana?"

"From the point of ordinary men," replied the Patriarch, "enlightenment and ignorance are two separate things. Wise men who thoroughly realise Mind-essence, know that they are of the same nature. This sameness of nature, that is, this non-duality of nature, is what is called 'true nature'; it neither decreases in the case of an ordinary man and ignorant person, nor increases in the case of an enlightened sage; it is undisturbed in an annoying situation, and is calm in Samadhi. It is neither eternal, nor not-eternal; it neither goes, nor comes, it is to be found neither in the interior, nor in exterior, nor in the space intervening between. It is beyond existence and nonexistence; its nature and its phenomena are always in a state of 'tathata'; it is both permanent and immutable. Such is the Norm."

Sit Kan asked, "You speak of it as beyond existence and non-existence. How do you differentiate it from the teaching of the heretics, who teach the same thing?"

The Patriarch replied: "In the teaching of the heretics, non-existence means the 'end' of existence, while existence is used in contrast with non-existence. What they mean by 'non-existence' is not actual annihilation, and what they mean by 'existence' really does not exist. What I mean by 'beyond existence and non-existence' is this: intrinsically it exists not, and at the present moment it is not annihilated. Such is the difference between my teaching and the teaching of the heretics. If you wish to know the essentials of my teaching, you should free yourself from all thought—good ones as well as bad ones—then your mind will be in a state of purity, ever calm and serene, the usefulness of which will be as apparent as the sands of the Ganges."

This preaching of the Patriarch, awoke Sit Kan to full enlightenment. He made obeisance to the Patriarch and bade him, adieu. Upon his return to the Palace, he reported to Their Majesties, what the Patriarch had said.

In that same year on the 3d day of the 9th Moon, an Edict was issued commending the Patriarch in the following terms:—

"On the ground of old age and poor health, the Patriarch declined our invitation to the Capital. Devoting his life, as he does, to the practice of

Buddhism for the benefit of us all, he is, indeed, 'a field of merit' for the nation. Following the example of Vimalakirti who recuperated in Vaisali, he widely spreads the Mahayana-teaching, transmitting the doctrines of the Dhyana School, expounding especially the 'non-dual' Dharma. Through the medium of Sit Kan to whom the Patriarch imparted the 'Buddha-knowledge,' we are fortunate enough to have an opportunity to understand clearly his teachings of Higher Buddhism. This must be due to the accumulated merit and our 'root of goodness' planted in past lives, otherwise we would not be contemporaries of His Eminence.

"In appreciation of the graciousness of the Patriarch, we find ourselves hardly able to express our gratitude. (As a token of our great regard for him) we present him herewith a Korean Mo-la robe and a crystal bowl. The Prefect of Shiu-chow is hereby ordered to renovate his monastery, and to convert his old residence into a temple which is to be named, Kwok-yen. By royal favor, etc., etc."

Chapter IX

Final Words and Death of the Patriarch

ON THE 1ST DAY of the 7th Moon, the Patriarch assembled his disciples and addressed them as follows:—

'I am going to leave this world by the 8th Moon. Should any of you have doubts about the teaching, please ask me soon, so that I may clear them away before I go. You may not find any one to teach you after I am gone." (The sad news moved many of them to tears. The Patriarch spoke to them at some length) and then added:—

"Under all circumstances you should free yourselves from attachment to objects; toward them your attitude should be neutral and indifferent. Let neither success nor failure, neither profit nor loss, worry you. Be ever calm and serene, modest and helpful, simple and dispassionate. The Dharma is non-dual as is the mind also. The Path is pure and above all 'form.' You are especially warned not to let the exercise for concentration of mind, fall into mere quiet thinking or into an effort to keep the mind in a blank state. The mind is by nature pure, there is nothing for us to crave or give up."

Realising that the Patriarch would pass away in the near future, Elder Fat-hoi after prostrating himself twice asked, "Sir, upon your entering into Parinirvana, who will be the inheritor of the robe and the (secret) Dharma?"

"(As for the Dharma) all my sermons from the time I preached in the Tai-fan Monastery up to now, may be copied out for circulation. You should take good care of it and hand it down from generation to generation for the salvation of all sentient beings. He who preaches in accordance with its teaching preaches the Orthodox Dharma. I have already made known to you, all the Dharma I know.

"As to the transmission of the robe, this practice is to be discontinued. Why? Because you all have implicit faith in my teaching, you are all free from doubts, therefore, you are all able to carry out the lofty object of our school. It is in accordance with the meaning of the stanza, handed down by Bodhidharma, the First Patriarch, that the robe be no longer handed down to posterity. The verse says:—

The object of my coming to China, Was to transmit the Dharma of deliverance to all under delusion. In five petals, the flower will be complete; Thereafter, fruit will come to maturity naturally.'

"Do your best each of you; go wherever circumstances lead you. Listen to this stanza:—

"With those who are sympathetic You may have discussion about Buddhism. As to those whose point of view differs from ours, Treat them

politely and try to make them happy. Disputes are alien to our school, They are incompatible with its spirit. p. 313 To be bigoted and to argue with others in disregard of this rule Is to subject one's Mind-essence to the bitterness of this mundane existence."

On the 8th day of the 7th Moon, the Patriarch suddenly gave an order to his disciples to get a boat ready for his return to Sun-chow, (his native place). They entreated him earnestly to remain where he was, but in vain.

"It is only natural," said the Patriarch, "death is the inevitable outcome of birth. Even the Buddhas as they appear in this world must manifest an earthly death before they enter Parinirvana. There will be no exception with me; my physical body must be laid down somewhere. Fallen leaves go back to the place where the root is."

On the 3rd day of the 8th Moon of the Year Kwai Tsau, the 2nd year of the Sin Tan Era, after eating with his disciples at the Kwok-yen Monastery (Sun-chow), the Patriarch spoke as follows:—

"Please sit down in order of seniority; I am going to say good bye to you. After my passing away, do not follow the worldly custom of crying and lamenting. Neither should messages of condolence be accepted, nor should mourning be worn. These things are contrary to orthodox teaching; he who does them is not my disciple. What you should do is to know your own mind and realise your own Buddha-nature, Which neither rests nor moves, neither becomes nor ceases to be, neither comes nor goes, neither affirms nor denies, neither remains nor departs. I repeat this to you that you may surely realise your Mind-essence. If you carry out my instructions after my death and practise them, then my going away will make no difference with you. On the other hand, if you go against my teachings, even if I remained with you, no benefit would be yours." Then he uttered this stanza:—

"Undisturbed and serene, the wise man practises no virtue; Self-possessed and dispassionate, he commits no sin; Calm and silent, he gives up seeing and hearing; Even and upright his mind abides nowhere."

Having uttered the stanza, he sat reverently until the third watch of the night, then he said abruptly, "I am going now," and in a moment passed away. At that time, a peculiar fragrance pervaded the room and a lunar rainbow appeared to link the earth and heaven; the trees in the grove turned pale and birds and animals cried mournfully.

In the 11th Moon of that year, the question of the Patriarch's resting place gave rise to a dispute among the government officials of Kwong-chow, Shiu-chow and Sun-chow, each arty being anxious to have the remains of the Patriarch removed to his own district. The Patriarch's disciples together with other Bhikkhus and laymen, took part in the controversy. Being unable to come to any agreement, they burnt incense and prayed to the Patriarch to indicate by the drift of the smoke the place he himself would like to rest. As the smoke turned directly to Tso-kai, the sacred shrine together with the inherited robe and bowl were accordingly removed back there on the 13th day of the 11th Moon.

Next year on the 25th day of the 7th Moon, the body was taken from the shrine and re-embalmed and placed in the stupa, and by imperial order, tablets were erected to record the life of the Patriarch.

The Patriarch inherited the robe when he was 24; he was ordained at 39; and died at the age of 76. For thirty-seven years he preached to the benefit of all sentient beings. Forty-three of his disciples inherited the Dharma; while those who attained (a measure of) enlightenment and thereby got out of the rut of the ordinary life were too many to be numbered. The robe transmitted by the First Patriarch, Bodhidharma, as the insignia of the Patriarchship, the Mo La robe and the crystal bowl presented by the Emperor Chung Chung, the Patriarch's image carved by Fong-pin, and other sacred things, were given into the care of the keeper of the stupa. They were to be kept permanently at Po-lam Monastery to guard the welfare of the temple. The Sutra spoken by the Patriarch was published and circulated to make known the principles of the Dhyana School. All these steps were taken for the prosperity of the "Three jewels," Buddha, Dharma and Sangha, as well as for the general welfare of all sentient beings.